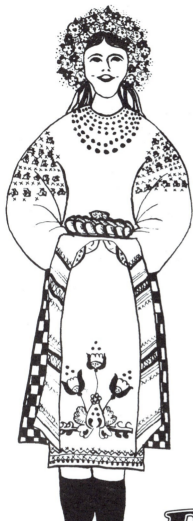

Baba's Cook Book
Volume 1

by Emily Linkiewich

FOREWORD

Ever since I was a young girl, I loved to help Mom in the kitchen. Growing up in a family of eleven, there always seemed to be something cooking at all times. From mouth-watering, fresh bread baked in the outdoor oven, to the pots of wholesome soups bubbling on the woodstoves, to roasters of creamed chicken, cabbage rolls and fresh berry pies tucked in the oven, these memories remain vivid in my mind and heart as everyone had an indirect part in the preparation of the meals.

Bringing in the milk and cream, gathering of eggs, picking garden vegetables and wild berries to butchering our own meat and poultry were never chores but an opportunity to help one another of the family and assist, indirectly, in the preparation of the meals.

My place on the farm was in the house, right in the kitchen, helping and learning the "secrets" and "basics" in making the food tasty and delicious. Over the years, I have always sought out good food and the recipes that came with them. Through the vast travels with my family, I have compiled a wealth of special recipes along with the traditional favorites that I grew up with. Many recipes here have been shared with you by friends, family and neighbours. With a common love of eating tasty food, I present to you — **"Baba's Cook Book"**.

Happy Cooking,
Emily Linkiewich

Additional Copies may be
obtained from:

Ukrainian Orthodox
Church of St. Anthony
6103 – 172 Street,
Edmonton, Alberta.
T6M 1C1.
Phone: (780) 487-2167
FAX : (780) 487-5446

Order form on page 159

DEDICATION

In thoughtful remembrance of my mother and her endearing skills she has passed on to me. To my children and their children's children, the very best of Baba's Cook Book.

E. L.

🎜🎜🎜🎜🎜🎜 Contents 🎜🎜🎜🎜🎜🎜

Traditional Ukrainian Christmas Eve Dishes 10

Traditional Ukrainian Easter Breakfast.................... 19

Soups.. 26

Meats and Casseroles.................................. 29

Fish 46

Breads. and Buns 54

Cakes and Tortes....................................... 61

Squares 90

Cookies 98

Pastry and Pies..108

Canning and Pickles 122

Icings 129

Salads...133

Desserts...138

Household Hints 146

Many thanks to family and friends for their contributions of favorite recipes.

Traditional Ukrainian
Christmas Eve Dishes

CHRISTMAS (RIZDVO)

The most beloved of all Ukrainian festivities is the Sviata Vecheria (Holy Supper). The supper differs from others in that twelve meatless dishes (symbolic of the twelve apostles) are prepared without animal fat, milk or milk products. This is done because Christmas is preceded by a period of fasting which ends on Christmas Day, after midnight or morning Church Service.

Respected and honoured customs pervade the house on Christmas Eve. The supper table is first strewn with a handful of hay (to remind us of the birth of Christ in a manger) then covered with an embroidered tablecloth. A braided round bread, kolach, symbolizing prosperity is placed in esteem in the center of the dining table; a sheaf of grain, the didukh, is set in the corner of the dining room, representative as a symbol of the gathering together of the family; a lit candle in the window invites those who are homeless; an extra place setting on the table is made for any member of the family who has deceased during the year; as soon as the children eagerly denote the appearance of the first star in the Eastern Heavens, the meal begins with the Lord's Prayer.

The eminently indispensable dish, Kutia, is raised in a spoon by the head of the family who invokes God's grace and greets all with the tradition Christmas greeting "Khrystos Rodyvsia!" (Christ is Born) to which the reply: "Slavim Yoho!" (Let us Glorify Him) is given.

After the Kutia, other delectable dishes are then served. Christmas Carols beginning with the oldest known koliady "Boh Predvichny" (God Eternal) are sung together. It is a night for family togetherness.

Traditional Ukrainian Christmas Eve Dishes

Kutia

Sauerkraut and Peas

Borsch

Jellied Fish

Fried Fish

Verenyky (Prune, Sauerkraut,
    Raisin and Poppy Seed Fillings)

Holubtsi

Cooked Beans

Beets with Mushrooms

Stewed Dry Fruits

Kolach

Pompushky

Beverage

TRADITIONAL DISHES FOR UKRAINIAN CHRISTMAS EVE

KUTIA (WHEAT)

2 cups wheat
½ cup sugar
½ cup honey

½ cup chopped nuts
½ cup poppy seed

Pick out foreign grains from wheat. Rinse well, and put wheat in a pan and dry in the oven for 1 hour at 225 degrees. Stir occasionally. Sprinkle with hot water, put in a sturdy sack and pound it with a rolling pin to loosen the outer layer of bran. Wash the wheat thoroughly by allowing the bran to rise to the top and remove it. Keep rinsing until the wheat is free from bran. Soak wheat overnight in 7 cups of water. Cook the wheat in the same water in which it was soaked. Stir frequently and add more water. Cook about 6 to 7 hours. About the last 2 hours it will thicken so stir often and cook on very low heat.

Wash poppy seed, pouring boiling water over it, rinsing off until it looks clean. Put it on the stove on simmer for about 10 minutes and keep the lid on. Grind the poppy seed in the blender or use the finest blade on the food chopper; also nice to leave it whole. Mix together cooked wheat, poppy seed and nuts, sugar and honey.

KUTIA (WHEAT DELICACY)

1 cup or more high grade wheat
   bran removed
½ cup or more poppy seed

water
salt
honey
chopped walnuts

Wash wheat in a sieve under running water. Soak overnight. Next day, simmer wheat covered with the same water for 6 hours. Stir occasionally. Add ½ tsp. salt before cooking is completed. Set aside.

Scald poppyseed and drain. Soak for 30 minutes in lukewarm water. Drain well and grind fine. Boil 1 part honey to 2 parts water. Cool. Combine syrup with wheat to make medium thin mixture. Stir in poppy seed and nuts. Serve either warm or chilled.

KUTIA (WHEAT)

2 cups wheat   3 quarts water

Pick out foreign grains from wheat. Rinse and soak overnight in lukewarm water. Cook wheat in the same water — add 1 tsp. salt. Simmer until very tender about 6 - 7 hours. More water will be needed, be careful not to burn. Meanwhile, scald ½ cup of poppy seed, drain well and simmer for a while (10 minutes). Poppy seed could be grinded on finest blade or in a blender. Add ½ cup honey and ½ cup sugar, ¼ cup chopped nuts if desired. Serve.

SAUERKRAUT AND PEAS

2 cups sauerkraut
½ cup water
½ cup dried peas
1 medium onion (chopped)
¼ cup cooking oil

2 tbsp. flour
salt and pepper to taste
1 small clove of garlic (crushed)

Soak peas overnight. Rinse peas and drain. Cover with fresh water and cook until tender 3-4 hours.

Rinse sauerkraut in cool water if too sour and drain it. Add ½ cup water and cook for 15-20 minutes.

Combine sauerkraut and peas, reserve liquid for sauce. Fry onions in oil till soft and light yellow in color. Sprinkle flour over the onions and brown very lightly. Pour the liquid and crushed garlic over the flour and onion. Stir constantly until sauce thickens. Add sauce to sauerkraut and peas. Stir, add salt and pepper to taste and simmer for 30 minutes. This should be of thick consistency and serve.

MOM'S SAUERKRAUT AND PEAS

1 quart sauerkraut
1½ quarts water

1 tbsp. salt
1 pkg. split peas

2 large onions
2 cups oil or butter

Rinse Kraut if too sour. Cover with water and salt and let boil, till tender. Thicken with 3 tbsp. flour and water. Pour about 1 cup Kraut juice into flour to avoid lumps.

Soak, 1 pkg. peas overnight. Rinse and drain. Cover with fresh water, 1 tsp. salt and cook until done (3-4 hours) adding more water if needed. Last hour of cooking peas will be quite thick. Do not add more water.

Fry ½ lb. butter, oil or margarine. Add 2 large onions, fry until onions look crisp. Remove from heat and serve with the sauerkraut and peas as soup.

BORSCH (Beet Soup)

2 cups beets cut into thin strips
1 medium onion (chopped)
½ cup carrots (cut into strips)
1 medium potato (small cubes)
1 tsp. dill weed
1 tsp. parsley chopped fine

2 cups shredded cabbage
9 cups water
2 tbsp. lemon juice
1½ tsp. salt
½ cup sour cream

Cover beets and carrots with water, add lemon juice and salt and simmer for ½ hour. Add the rest of vegetables. Cook ½ hour longer and pour cream and serve.

BORSCH (Beet soup)

1 cup carrots (diced)
1 cup celery (chopped)
2½ cups beets
1 cup cabbage shredded
1 medium onion chopped fine
1 tbsp. salt

1½ tbsp. lemon juice
7 cups water
2 cups tomato juice or
1 can tomato soup
2 tbsp. corn starch
3 tbsp. cooking oil

Grate beets on medium grater and add carrots, celery, cabbage, onion, salt, lemon juice. Bring to a boil and simmer for ½ hr. Add corn starch in ½ cup water — slowly add to borsch. Bring to a boil. Serve hot.

JELLIED FISH

3 lb. raw fish
3 cups water
1 small onion, diced

2½ tsp. salt
⅛ tsp. pepper
1 pkg. unflavored gelatin

Clean and wash fish thoroughly in cold water. Cut into serving pieces and place into sauce pan. Add water and bring to a boil. Add onion and salt. Simmer slowly for 1 hour. Lift the fish out carefully into a platter. Strain juice. Soak gelatin in 1 tbsp. cold water. Add to the juice and stir well. Now pour juice over fish and let set at least 6 to 12 hours.

STUFFED FISH

5 lb. salmon or any other
    fish of your choice
1 medium chopped onion
1 cup celery chopped fine
¼ cup cooking oil
2 cups dry bread crumbs
½ tsp. salt

⅛ tsp. pepper
½ tsp. sage
¼ cup water

Scale and clean the fish. Fry onion and celery in oil. Combine with all the remaining ingredients. Stuff salmon. Brush outer surface with oil. Bake on a large pan at 400 degrees allowing 10 minutes for every inch of fish.

Serve on hot platter garnished with parsley and lemon wedges.

PICKLED HERRING

4 salt herrings (2 with milts)
1 medium onion sliced
1 tbsp. cooking oil

1 cup vinegar
1 tsp. mixed spices
¼ cup water

Wash herring well and soak overnight changing the water 3 or 4 times (cold water only). Wash thoroughly again and cut into serving pieces. Pack in jars with layers of onion, fish, milt and spices. Pour vinegar oil and water over the herring and seal. Store in refrigerator overnight before serving.

PAN FRIED FISH

Wash fish, beat egg lightly, add salt and pepper to ½ cup flour.

Dust fish in flour and seasoning then dip in egg and fry in hot oil or butter. Crush 2 cloves of garlic, add ¼ cup water and pour over fish. Let simmer for 15-20 minutes and serve hot.

VARENYKY (PYROHY)

4 cups flour	2 eggs
1 cup warm water	2 tsp. salt
2 tbsp. cooking oil	

Beat the eggs and add to the warm water and oil. Blend well, then add flour and salt. Knead dough until smooth and soft. Cover dough and let rest for 30 minutes, roll out thin. Cut into squares or rounds.

Place a teaspoon filling on each piece, pinch edges well together to seal. Drop into boiling salted water and boil for about eight minutes. Strain in a colonder and pour 1 cup cold water over them. Drain, place in dish, sprinkle with oil toss gently to coat evenly. Fry chopped onions in oil. Spread over pyrohy and serve hot.

FILLING FOR PYROHY

Potato filling

2 cups mashed potatoes	salt and pepper to taste
½ cup cottage cheese.	½ tbsp. onion chopped

Saute onion in oil, season and add to potato and cheese. Mix well.

Plum filling

½ cup water	1 cup prunes
¼ tsp. cinnamon	sugar to taste

Bring prunes to boil. Let cool, remove stones and chop fine.

Sauerkraut filling

Cook 2 cups sauerkraut. Drain and press out water. Chop 1 small onion and fry in 4 tbsp. cooking oil. Add to kraut.

Poppy Seed Filling

½ cup prepared poppy seed, scalded and ground fine. Pinch of salt and pepper. 2 tablespoons sugar. Mix well.

Raisin Filling

Cook 1 cup raisins and drain well. Mix ¼ cup sugar and ½ tsp. of cornstarch into each dumpling, seal well.

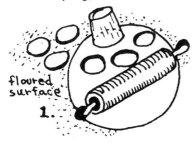

floured surface
1.

2.
dip fingers in flour
3.

HOLUBTSI STUFFED CABBAGE ROLL MEATLESS

Remove hard core of 3 lb. cabbage. Simmer, covered, removing outer leaves as they wilt. Do not overcook. Line casserole with smallest and damaged leaves. Wash 2 oz. dried mushrooms. Simmer in 3 cups water for 1 hour. Strain stock and chop mushrooms. Saute 1 cup onions (chopped) in ½ cup vegetable oil. Partly cook 2 cups rice in 3 cups mushroom stock and water. Add mushrooms and ½ the onion. Overseason rice with salt and pepper. Form holubtsi and arrange in layers in casserole. Add 2 cups water or tomato juice (to barely show). Sprinkle with ½ cup vegetable oil and remaining onion. Bake, covered, at 350 degrees for 1 hour. To form holubtsi. Place 1 tbsp. rice mixture on leaf. Fold sides toward centre starting at thin outer edge; roll up loosely.

Holubtsi can be reheated in the casserole or sauteed individually. Buckwheat can be substituted for rice. Serve with sour cream or favorite sauce.

Holubtsi are usually the fifth course in the traditional Ukrainian Christmas Eve Supper preceded by Kutia, Borsch, Fish, and Varenyky. Cabbage was among the staple vegetables in Old Ukraine and could be stored through the winter. Prepared carefully, cabbage can be a delicacy.

BIB

1 lb. broad beans   1 med. onion, chopped
¼ cup oil

Soak broad beans overnight. Drain, add fresh water to cover and simmer for 2 hours. Drain, add 1 onion and set aside for 5 to 10 minutes. Fry remaining onion in oil and add to the broad beans.

MASHED BEANS (Kalocheni Fasali)

1 lb. white navy beans   3 cloves garlic (minced)
1 medium onion (chopped fine)   salt and pepper to taste
¼ cup cooking oil

Rinse beans and soak overnight. Drain, add fresh water to cover beans, and slowly cook about three hours or in pressure cooker for 30 minutes. Drain and mash. Saute onions and seasonings in oil. Add to beans, stir in garlic. Serve hot.

BEETS AND PEDPENKY (MUSHROOMS)

Cook beets, cut in thin strips. Cook pedpenky or mushrooms. 4 cups beets/2 cups mushrooms. Heat ½ cup cooking oil, crush 3 cloves garlic minced, mix together with oil, mushrooms and beets. Add ½ tsp. salt. Simmer for 15 min. or until beet mixture is hot. Remove from stove. Beets will lose color if heated too much. Stir and serve.

BEETS WITH MUSHROOMS

In ½ cup cooking oil, gently fry 1 medium onion, finely chopped. Combine 4 cups cooked beets, finely sliced into strips.

1 cup sliced cooked mushrooms	3 cloves crushed garlic
1 tbsp. sugar	2 tbsp. vinegar
¼ tsp. salt	¼ tsp. pepper

Add to onions and stir gently. Chill overnight in refrigerator. Serve cold as a vegetable or salad. Makes 8 servings.

TRADITIONAL KOLACH

1 tsp. sugar	1 tbsp. salt
½ cup lukewarm water	½ cup sugar
2 pkgs. yeast	4 tbsp. oil
2½ cups water	8½ cups all purpose flour
4 eggs (beaten)	

Dissolve sugar in water, add yeast and let rise for 10 minutes. Combine the softened yeast with lukewarm water, eggs, salt, sugar, and oil. Mix in the flour and knead until it is smooth and dough leaves the hand. The dough should be a little stiffer than for bread. Cover and let rise in warm place until double in bulk. Punch down and let rise again.

This recipe will make 2 round Kalachi. Divide the dough into 4 equal portions and shape each portion as directed below. Grease a round pan 9¼ by 2 inches. Take one portion of the dough and divide it into 5 equal parts. Roll out 3 parts about 36 inches long with the thickness twice the size of a pencil. Braid these 3 lengths. Join ends and place in a pan leaving a 1 inch space around the edge of the pan. Now take the other 2 lengths and entwine, starting at the centre and working from left to right. Now turn your entwined length around and repeat. Join ends and place in the pan in the one inch space next to the braid. This is the base for the Kalachi.

Take the second portion and make 6 equal pieces of dough, roll out each piece to about 38 inches long and make it the same thickness as above. Now take 2 lengths and entwine, starting at the centre working from left to right. Turn and repeat. Use the remaining 4 lengths, repeat the entwining by two as above. Now you have 3 entwined lengths. Starting at centre and working from left to right take the 2 entwined lengths that are on the left and cross them over onto the lengths that are on the right. Repeat until that half is entwined. Turn and repeat.

Neatly join the entwined length and place on top of the base already in the pan, making sure that the length is placed in an even circle. Brush the base with water lightly. Press it down lightly, so it will stick to the base. Put in a warm place to rise until almost double in size. Glaze with 1 beaten egg and bake at 350 degrees for 45 minutes or until done. Work the other two the same as first.

POMPUSHKY

3 pkgs. yeast
1 tsp. sugar
2 cups lukewarm water
1 cup scalded milk
¼ cup butter or margarine

4 eggs
1 tsp. salt
10 cups flour
1 cup warm honey
¾ cup oil

Dissolve 1 tsp. of sugar in 1 cup lukewarm water, add the yeast and let stand 10 minutes in a warm place.

In a large bowl, place the flour, making a well in the middle. Beat the eggs and the oil, melted margarine, honey, milk, balance of water and salt. Add this to the flour. Add yeast and mix. Knead in a bowl for 10 minutes. This dough should be soft. Cover and let rise in a warm place until double in bulk. Punch down, knead a few times and let rise again. Take small egg-sized pieces of dough, flatten each or roll ½ inch thick. Place a generous portion of the filling in the centre, bring the edges together and press to seal securely. All the edges must be free of filling. Place pompushky on a lightly floured board and let rise 1 hour. Deep fry in oil for about 3 minutes, turning them to brown evenly on both sides. Drain on absorbent paper.

Poppy Seed Filling

1 cup ground poppy seed
⅓ cup honey
1 tsp. grated lemon rind
1 egg white

Mix poppy seeds, honey and lemon rind in a small bowl. Beat the egg white until stiff and fold into the mixture.

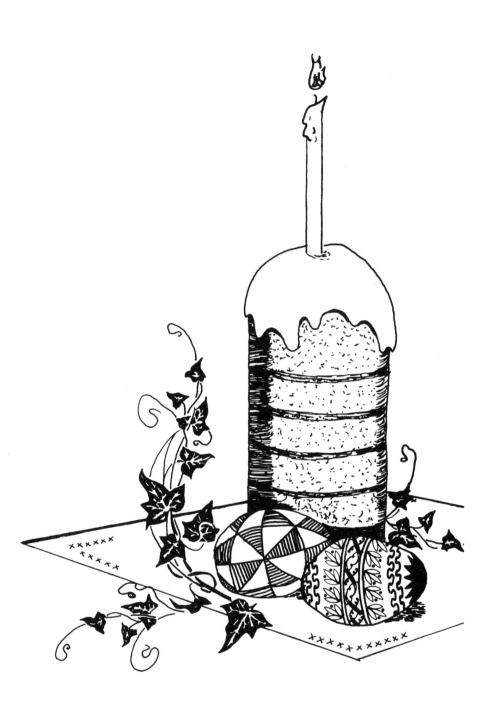

Traditional Ukrainian
🔲🔲🔲🔲 Easter Breakfast 🔲🔲🔲🔲

VELYKDEN (EASTER)

The observance of the Great Lent six weeks before Easter initiates the duration of time which spiritual purification, personal retreat, and fasting are observed. Confession and Holy Communion are then partaken by the faithful so as to cleanse and purify the soul.

One of the most beautiful traditions of the Ukrainian people is the writing of decorated Easter eggs called "Pysanky." In pagan times, pysanky symbolized the release of the earth from the bonds of winter and the arrival of spring. They are associated with mythical beliefs and magical powers. After the coming of Christianity, the pysanky were then associated with the Resurrection, a symbol of eternal life. A customary exchange or gift of a pysanka at Easter is something to be cherished and loved.

At break of dawn on Easter Sunday a special Resurrection Service is held which includes a procession around the church. The most joyful aspect of the service is the heralding of the resurrected Christ in the singing of Khrystos Voskres (Christ is Risen). With the conclusion of the service, weather permitting, all exit to outside the church and form a circle. The embroidered covered baskets containing an array of meticulously prepared foods are proudly exhibited in front of each family. A candle is lit and placed in each basket. Anxious children peer from behind the colorful woven vessels to watch the priest bless the food with Holy water. We now extend the traditional Easter greeting "Khrystos Voskres" (Christ is Risen), to which the reply is "Voistyno Voskres" (Truly He is Risen).

Families return home to break the long fast with a delicious meal. After the Lord's Prayer and the traditional Easter salutation, a blessed egg is cut into pieces, one for everyone present and then a little of each type of food from the basket is consumed. Following this, larger portions are served from a variety of prepared dishes.

This observance not only expresses the families unity but fills their religious aspirations and beliefs in the preservation of a glorious time-honored ritual and tradition.

Traditional Ukrainian Easter Breakfast

Blessed Boiled Eggs

Paska

Babka

Ham

Pork Roast

Kyshka (buckwheat sausage)

Kobassa (ham sausage)

Salteson

Easter Syrnyk

Beet and Horseradish Relish

Butter

Pysanky and Krashanky (decorated and
   colored eggs for ornamentation)

HARD BOILED EGGS

6 eggs.

Cover with cold water, turn heat to high until steaming. Turn heat to low for 15 minutes. Cool quickly under cold running water.

PASKA

1 tsp. sugar	6 eggs, beaten
1 cup lukewarm water	⅓ cup sugar
1 pkg. yeast	½ cup melted butter
3 cups scalded milk, lukewarm	1 tbsp. salt
5 cups flour	9 to 10 cups flour

Dissolve the sugar in the lukewarm water and sprinkle the yeast over it, let it stand for 10 minutes. Combine the softened yeast along with the lukewarm milk and 5 cups of flour. Beat well until smooth. Cover and let the batter rise in a warm place until light and bubbly. Add the beaten eggs, sugar, melted butter, and salt; mix thoroughly. Stir in enough flour to make a dough that is neither too soft nor too stiff. Knead the dough until the dough no longer sticks to the hand. Turn the dough on a floured board and knead until it is smooth and satiny. Place the mixture in a bowl, cover, and let it rise in a warm place until double in bulk. Punch down and let dough rise again.

Divide the dough into three equal parts. Set 1 part aside for the ornamentations. Shape the other 2 parts into 2 round loaves. Set each in a greased, round pan. Now cut the set aside piece into two sections. The main ornament on the paska is usually the cross. Roll 2 long tube-like strips and trim the ends. Place these over the top of the loaf, crossing one another evenly. Shape the trimmed dough into twisted swirls or rosettes, and arrange them symmetrically between the arms of the cross. Use sharp greased scissors to make fine petals on the rosettes. Once the cross is placed on the loaf, the remaining ornamentations are left to the creativity and artistic imagination of the person baking the bread.

Set the loaves in a warm place until they are almost double in bulk. Be careul not to let the loaves rise longer than necessary because the ornaments will lose their definition. Brush very carefully with a beaten egg diluted wth 2 tablespoons of water. Bake in a moderately hot oven (400°F) for about 15 minutes, then lower the temperature to 350°F, and continue baking for 40 minutes or until done. Avoid browning the top too deeply and if necessary use a piece of tin foil to cover the top for the last 10 minutes of baking as the finished loaf should be light honey in color.

A SUCCESSFUL BABKA

1 cup milk	1 tsp. salt
⅓ cup flour	1⅓ cups icing sugar
2 tsp. sugar	1 cup butter, melted
3 pkgs. yeast	Grated rind and juice of 1 orange
12 egg yolks	5½ - 6 cups flour
2 whole eggs	1 cup raisins

In the following recipe the sponge is made with a base of a hot milk — flour paste. This method gives a finer texture to Babka and helps to retain its freshness longer.

Bring the milk to a boil and remove from stove. Add the hot milk gradually to the 1/3 cup flour and beat thoroughly until smooth and free of lumps. If necessary, strain or press the mixture through a seive. Cool it to lukewarm. Dissolve the sugar in the lukewarm water. Sprinkle the yeast over it, and let stand until yeast is softened. Combine yeast with flour, milk mixture, beat well, cover and let it rise in a warm place until light and bubbly. Beat the egg yolks and the whole eggs together along with the salt, add the sugar gradually and continue beating until light. Stir in butter, orange juice and rind. Combine this mixture with the sponge and mix well. Stir in enough flour to make a very soft dough and knead by working the dough over and up continually for 10 minutes. The usual method of kneading does not apply to Babka dough. This dough is very soft. When raisins are used, they should be added after dough is kneaded. Cover and let rise in a warm place until double in bulk. Punch down and let rise again. Punch down and let rise once more. Prepare tall, round pans by buttering them generously, with soft butter and sprinkling them lightly with fine crumbs or line with wax paper. Fill pans 1/3 full. Cover and let dough rise in a warm place until dough reaches the top of the pan.

Brush the loaves gently with a beaten egg diluted with 2 tbsp. of water. Bake in a moderate oven 375°F for about 10 minutes, then lower the temperature at about 325°F and bake for 30 minutes. Then again lower temp. to 275°F and continue baking for 15-20 min. The baking period will depend on the size of the loaves. If Babka is turning dark cover with aluminum foil. Remove baked loaves from the oven and let them stand in the pans for 5-10 min. Take each loaf out very carefully. Tip it gently on a cloth covered pillow. Do not cool loaves on a hard surface. Any careless handling of the baked Babka may cause it to fall or settle. As the loaves are cooling change the position very gently a few times to prevent settling. Babka is always sliced in rounds across the loaf.

BABKA

2 cups sugar
1 cup butter
2 cups raisins
5 cups milk, scalded and cooled

14½ cups flour
20 egg yolks
1 tsp. salt
3 pkgs. yeast
2 oranges — juice & rind

Soak yeast in milk and add some flour and let rise till bubbly. Cream butter, sugar, egg yolks. Combine with yeast mixture. Add more flour, raisins, orange. Dough should be soft. Let rise again. Grease tall tins and fill 1/3 full. Let rise until dough rises to top. Bake in moderate oven for about 1 hour or until done.

Babka should be handled very carefully when taken out of the container. It should be laid on a soft, covered cushion or pillow. Change position as Babka cools.

UKRAINIAN EASTER BABKA

½ cup lukewarm water
2 pkgs. yeast
1 tsp sugar
2 cups scalded milk
½ lb. butter melted
1 tbsp. salt
Flour to make soft dough
   (about 7 cups or more)

1¼ cup sugar
5 whole eggs
10 yolks
juice and rind of 1 orange
1 cup golden raisins

Dissolve the sugar in lukewarm water, sprinkle the yeast over it, let stand 10 minutes. Beat the eggs and the egg yolks adding the sugar, a little at a time. Add the salt, orange juice, milk, rind and the yeast mixture to the beaten eggs.

Blend well, and gradually mix in the flour, adding the melted butter a little at a time, to make a soft dough. Knead dough until it no longer clings to hands. Cover and let rise in warm place until double in bulk. Knead and let rise again as before. Grease tall tins and coat with bread crumbs (coffee or Crisco tins are nice). Form dough into a ball enough to fill ⅓ of the container. Let rise in a warm place until the dough barely reaches the top. Bake in a preheated oven 350 degrees and bake for 25-30 minutes then lower heat to 300 degrees. Brush babka with 1 egg beaten and a little water added before baking.

Babka should be handled very carefully when taken out of the container. It should be laid on a soft, covered cushion or pillow. Change position as Babka cools.

BABKA WITH ICING SUGAR

2 pkgs. yeast
2 cups milk scalded
15 egg yolks
1½ cups icing sugar
1 tsp. salt

½ lb. white raisins
grated rind and juice of
  1 orange
8 cups flour or more
1 cup melted butter

Dissolve yeast in lukewarm milk. Add 1 cup flour and beat until smooth. Cover, set in warm place and let rise until double in bulk. Beat egg yolks until light adding icing sugar and orange juice gradually while beating. Combine with yeast mixture. Mix in rest of flour and salt. Knead dough until blended. Let rise until double in bulk.

Put into tall round pans or cans lined with wax paper. Fill cans ½ full. Let rise in warm place until full. Brush with beaten egg diluted with 2 tbsp. water.

Bake in slow oven 300 degrees for about 45-60 minutes.

Babka should be handled very carefully when taken out of the containers and should be laid on a soft, covered cushion to cool. Change positions as Babka cools.

CURED HAM

10-12 lbs. pork shoulder or leg of pork
¾ lbs. brown sugar
3 cups water
pickling spice

¾ cup pickling salt
2½ tbsp. saltpeter

Bring sugar, spices and water to a boil. Remove from heat and cool. Then add salt and saltpeter. Mix well until thoroughly dissolved. Add enough water to cover your ham. Let stand in brine in a crock or enamel roaster in a cool place for a week turning once or twice. Then remove from brine and wash thoroughly and roast.

MUSTARD GLAZE HAM

Ready to serve ham
6-8 lbs. ham
whole cloves to taste
¼ cup prepared mustard

½ cup brown sugar
6 oz. can frozen orange juice
  (undiluted)

Score fat on the ham. Stick cloves in here and there. Combine mustard, brown sugar and orange juice and pour over the ham. Place in at 400°F for 20 minutes until shiny and golden. Baste 2 or 3 times during baking. Serve hot or cold.

KYSHKA BUCKWHEAT SAUSAGE

Bring to a boil 4 cups of water and 2 tsp. salt. Add 2 cups clean buckwheat and cook for ¼ hour. Add ¼ cup fat which you may cut off a ham. Minced garlic and 1 tsp. pepper.

Mix well and cool. Spoon into clean casing and roast in an open pan where you have added ½ cup lard and 1 cup water.

Prick sausage with a needle to let air out. Do not handle sausage too much when roasting as it may burst the casing.

HOMEMADE SAUSAGE

4 lbs. pork
1 lb. ham
5 tsp. salt

2 tsp. pepper
1-2 cups water
2-3 cloves (crushed garlic)

Soak casings for 15-20 minutes. Rinse well with cold water. Grind meat on coarse blade. Mix everything together and stuff casings. Bake in the oven till done 350°F (1-1½ hours).

SALCHISON

This is an old country specialty that is worth reviving. It is a combination of a variety of pork meats made into a press loaf. When properly prepared, salchison is truly a great delicacy.

2 pigs ear
2 tbsp. salt
2 pork kidneys
1 clove garlic
1 med. carrot, chopped

5 peppercorns
1 pork tongue
½ tsp. saltpeter
1 med. onion, chopped
1 bay leaf
1 pigs stomach

1 pork heart
1 lb. pork liver
½ lb. pork shoulder
1 cup fresh pig or calf
   blood

Singe, scrape and wash the pigs ears very thoroughly. Cut the heart into halves, remove the veins and arteries and wash it well under running water. Cut away the roots from the tongue, scrub, skin and wash it well. Split kidneys into halves, remove the fat and tubes, and wash thoroughly under running water. Cut the pork shoulder into several pieces.

Place all the cleaned meat in a large kettle, cover with cold water. Bring to a boil and skim. Add the vegetables, spices and salt. Cover and simmer until the meat is tender. When done, add the liver and saltpetre. Continue cooking till liver is done. Strain the meat and save the stock. Remove all the vegetables, spices and bone from the meat. Cut the meat into small pieces. Do not discard the ear gristle. Chop it into small pieces.Chop the skin and fat of the pork shoulder finely.Crush the garlic and add it to 2 cups of hot stock. Strain the stock and pour it over the meat. Season to taste. Finally add strained blood and thoroughly mix. Have the pig's stomach cleaned and washed, soak in salty water for a while, ½ hr. Fill stomach with the meat mixture three quarters full and sew the edge securely. Do not overfill. Place in a large kettle cover with hot water and simmer under cover for 30-40 minutes. Test for readiness by pricking it with a darning needle. If the juice is clear with no blood coloring, the meat is ready.

When done, remove the salchison to a plate and let it cool slightly. Place a board over the loaf and weigh it down with a light weight. It must not be too heavy or the loaf will crack. Refrigerate overnight and serve chilled.

EASTER SYRNYK (CHEESE CAKE)

The following Syrnyk is served with the main course at Easter time.

1 pound dry cottage cheese
4 egg yolks

1 tbsp. melted butter
1 whole egg
1 tbsp. sugar

Press the cottage cheese through a sieve. Beat the egg yolks and the whole egg together until very light and creamy. Combine with the cheese and beat well. Spoon the mixture into a well buttered baking dish. Bake in a slow oven 300-325°F for 45 minutes or until a tooth pick inserted comes out clean. Cool thoroughly before serving.

EASTER MACARONI CASSEROLE

2½ cups egg noodle
¼ cup sugar
½ tsp. salt
¼ tsp. cinnamon

½ cup raisins washed well
3 eggs·
1 cup scalded milk
½ cup butter

Cook noodles in salted water until almost done. Drain well. Add melted butter and mix well. Add raisins and the mixture of sugar, salt, cinnamon, beaten eggs and the cooled milk to macaroni.

Place in a well buttered casserole and bake in a moderate oven 350°F about 30 minutes.

BEET RELISH

Wash 12 large beets. Cook and remove skin. Grate or put the beets through a food chopper. Wash horseradish and scrape or put through food chopper enough to make approximately 2 cups. Mix the horseradish with the beets.

4 cups vinegar
1 cup sugar or more
1 tsp. salt.

Bring brine to a boil and pour over the beets and horseradish. Mix well and fill into sterilized jars and place jars in boiler of hot water and boil for 20 minutes or put in containers and freeze.

STUDENETZ JELLY PIGS FEET

3 pigs feet
3 pork hocks
1 tbsp. salt

4 stalks celery and leaves
1 medium onion
1 clove garlic
1 bay leaf

Scrape and wash the pigs feet very thoroughly. Cut the feet in half lengthwise. Wash the hocks. Place the meat in a large kettle and add salt, cover with cold water and bring to a boil. Skim, cover and simmer very slowly. This is very important. Rapid boiling will make the broth milky. After 4 hours of boiling, add the whole vegetables and spices. Continue cooking slowly until the meat comes off the bones easily. Separate the meat from the bones, strain the juice and pour over the meat. Chill thoroughly. Meat and juice has to set like jelly.

Before serving, remove the fat from the top. Serve in slices and garnish with sprigs of parsley.

▣▣▣▣▣▣▣▣▣Soups▣▣▣▣▣▣▣▣▣

KEN'S CRABAPPLE BORSCH

Take 2 cups of washed, quartered, and cored ripe crabapple
3 cups water
3 tbsp. honey
Bring to a boil and add 2 tbsp. flour to thicken, ½ cup cream
Serve hot or cold. Deliciously refreshing.

CHICKEN SOUP WITH NOODLES

| 1 boiling fowl | small onion, diced | 4 qts water |
| 2 medium carrots | salt to taste | parsley root and green dill |

Singe and wash fowl thoroughly. Trim excess fat and bring slowly to a boil in salted water. Skim. Boil slowly for two hours. Add carrot, onion and boil for fifteen minutes more. Add parsley and dill. You can strain and serve clear with egg noodles or add noodles to soup stock.

Egg Noodles

| 2 eggs | 1 tbsp. milk |
| 1 ½ cups flour | ¼ tsp. salt |

Mix the ingredients into a smooth, stiff dough. Let rest for ten minutes, then, on a floured board, roll out as thin as possible. Let dry for a few minutes. Dust with flour. Cut in strips 1 ½ inches wide. Place on top of each other and cut into fine shreds. Boil for ten minutes in salted water, strain, and serve with chicken soup.

OLD TIME DUMPLINGS

1 ½ tbsp. shortening	1 tbsp. baking powder
1 tsp. salt	1 ¾ cups flour
1 cup milk	parsley flakes if desired

Cut shortening into dry ingredients (as you would for pie crust). Add milk. Stir. Drop by spoonfuls into broth that is boiling rapidly. Cover tightly. Cook for 14 minutes. Serve.

POTATO SOUP WITH GRAVY

3 good sized potatoes, diced	1 large onion
½ lb. bacon	4 tbsp. flour, browned in a heavy skillet
6 cups cold water	salt to taste

Let potatoes boil until cooked. Fry bacon and onions. Brown flour in a heavy skillet, or add 1 tbsp. shortening and brown. Combine with potatoes. Stir. Add bacon and onions. Serve.

POTATO AND DUMPLING SOUP

2 qts. potatoes, diced   ½ lb. bacon   dry cottage cheese
1 med. onion, diced   salt to taste   —optional

Cover diced potatoes with water; add salt. Cook until almost done. Fry diced bacon and onion. Set aside.

Dumplings

1 egg   1 tsp. milk
¾ cup flour   ¼ tsp. salt

Mix the ingredients into a smooth, stiff dough. Let rise 10 minutes. Pinch little pieces off dough and place on a tea towel. When all dough has been used up, have the potato water boiling. Drop the dough into the soup, boil until dough is cooked. Thicken soup with flour mixed in a little water. Cook for 5 minutes. Stir in the fried bacon and onions. Serve with dry cottage cheese.

SPRING BEETS (BORSCH)

10 young beets, stalks and leaves   2 garlic cloves, diced
6 cups water, to just cover   2 tbsp. chopped dill
2 tsp. salt   ½ cup peas, fresh
1 onion, diced   ½ cup beans
2 tbsp. parsley   ½ cup potatoes, diced
2 tbsp. lemon juice   1 tbsp. sugar
½ cup broad beans   1 cup sour or sweet cream

Scrub the beets thoroughly — but do not peel — rinse leaves and stalks under running water. Set leaves aside, dice beets and stalks. Add water, salt, and lemon juice. Bring to a boil, add diced leaves and the rest of the vegetables. Do not over-cook. Lemon juice or vinegar will give beets a nice, deep red color. Last of all, add cream and serve.

STANDARD BORSCH (BEET SOUP)

1 ½ pounds soup meat with bone   2 tbsp. lemon juice
½ cup diced string beans   10-12 cups cold water
    or cooked white beans   2-3 cups shredded cabbage
1 medium onion, chopped   2 medium carrots, cut in strips
¾ cup tomatoes or   3 medium beets, cut in thin strips
    tomato juice (optional)   1 clove garlic, crushed
1 medium potato, diced   ½ cup celery, thinly sliced
½ cup sour cream   chopped dill, salt to taste

Cover the meat with cold water, add the salt, bring slowly to the boiling point, then skim. Cover and simmer 1 ½ hours. Add vegetables. Cook until tender. Add cream just before serving.

CHICKEN SOUP

Wash chicken thoroughly and cut up for serving. Cover the meat with cold water and add salt to taste. Bring slowly to a boil and skim. Simmer until meat is almost tender. Add vegetables such as carrots, celery, onion, and parsley. The broth may be served with one of the following: egg noodles or steamed rice. For a nice variation, add 1 cup stewed tomatoes.

LLOYD'S RHUBARB SOUP

4 cups rhubarb, diced	1 tsp. salt	2 cups potatoes, diced
¼ cup onion, diced	1 cup cream	¼ cup dill and parsley
½ cup celery, diced		

Wash rhubarb and vegetables. Dice. Cover with water; add salt. Bring to a boil. Simmer 15 minutes. Remove from stove.

Add cream and serve.

VEGETABLE CHOWDER

⅓ cup diced bacon	3 tbsp. green pepper
¼ cup chopped onion	4 cups hot milk
1 cup diced celery	1 cup frozen peas
1 cup diced potatoes	2 tbsp. flour
1 cup water	1 cup diced carrots
2 tbsp. butter	2 tsp. salt
	2 tbsp. chopped parsley

Fry bacon until crisp. Add onion and cook until yellow. Add celery, potatoes, carrots, water, salt, and pepper. Cover, cook 20 minutes or until vegetables are tender. Add milk and peas. Cream butter and flour together. Add a little of the hot mixture and stir until smooth. Add to vegetable mixture. Cover and simmer 5 minutes. Add parsley. Serves 6 to 8.

MANHATTEN CLAM CHOWDER SOUP

1 can baby clams	2 tbsp. butter	1 stalk celery
1 medium onion	1 can tomatoes	3 potatoes
2 carrots	1 clove garlic	seasoning to taste

Melt butter in the pot, then add diced onion and garlic. Fry for 5 minutes. Add your diced vegetables to the onions and garlic. Pour in enough water to cover the vegetables. Bring to a boil and let cook until potatoes, carrots, and celery are tender. Add juice from clams and then add the tomatoes and clams. Heat again. Add seasoning to taste.

BORSCH MEATLESS

Simmer 1 oz. mushrooms in 3 cups water for 1 hour. Strain through cloth. Save stock. Wash mushrooms thoroughly and save. Saute 1 chopped onion in 2 tbsp. vegetable oil until golden. Add 2 medium beets, 1 carrot, and 1 stalk celery, all chopped. Cook 5 minutes. Add 6 cups boiling water, 1 whole onion, bay leaf, 10 peppercorns, and 1 tbsp. lemon juice or vinegar, and 2 tbsp. tomato paste. Simmer 15 minutes. Add 1 cup chopped cabbage. Simmer 20 minutes. Remove the whole onion, peppercorns and bay leaf. Add mushroom stock and salt to taste. Cool to let flavors "Marry". Serve cold or reheat. Add mushrooms and 2 tbsp. of sour cream to each serving, or make traditional "curshka" of sauteed onions and mushrooms in thin dough dumplings. Serves 8 to 10.

⑤⑤Meats and Casseroles ⑤⑤

VARENYKY (PYROGI) (DUMPLINGS)

Dough: Mix 2 cups flour with 1 tsp. salt. Add 1 egg and ⅔ cup cool water. Knead lightly. Cover with lid and set aside.

Potato Filling: Mash 4 large cooked potatoes. Add 1 large chopped onion sauted in ½ cup vegetable oil. Season with salt and pepper. Cool.

Saurkraut Filling: Rinse 1½ lbs. saurkraut with hot water to remove salt. Rinse cold. Squeeze dry. Chop fine. Saute 1 large onion in ⅓ cups oil. Add saurkraut. Saute covered, for 10 minutes. Season. Cool.

Cheese Filling: Combine 2 cups farm cheese, 4 oz. cream cheese, 1 egg, salt; add a little sour cream if mixture is too dry.

Fruit Filling: Fresh berries, pitted cherries, plums, or stewed prunes can be used. Sprinkle lightly with cornstarch and sugar mixed in equal parts.

To Form Varenyky (Pyrogi)

Roll dough thin. Cut round with inverted water glass.

Hold round in palm, face up, place spoonful of filling in centre. Fold in half.

Press edges to seal.

Lay on dry, clean kitchen towel and cover.

To cook: Drop into large pot of boiling water, a few at a time. Boil rapidly about 4 minutes. Lift out and rinse with hot water. Drain. Coat with melted butter. Keep hot. Serve with sour cream.

Varenyky are delicious as leftovers. Saute in butter and onion until golden and crisp.

floured surface
1.

2.

dip fingers in flour
3.

CABBAGE ROLLS

1 medium head sour cabbage
   if too sour, rinse leaves
2 cups uncooked rice, rinsed

1 medium onion, diced
½ cup oil or other shortening

Steam rice in 1 tsp. salted water until about half cooked. Fry onions in oil, add to the rice, mix well. Cool a while. Tear cabbage leaves to desired size and put 1 tbsp. rice in each leaf, roll tightly. Place in casserole or roaster. Before baking, add ½ tsp. salt to 2 cups boiled water and pour over the rolls. Then add ½ cup oil or shortening over rolls. Bake for 1½ hours at 325°F or until a fork twists in roll and breaks it easily.

To Form Holubtsi

Place 1 tbsp. of rice mixture on leaf. Fold sides toward center. Starting at thin outer edge, roll up securely.

BEET LEAF HOLUBTSI

2 cups cold water

1 cup rice
1 tsp. salt

Bring the water, salt, and rice (washed) to a boil, cover and steam for 10 minutes on low heat. Fry ¼ cup onions in ½ cup butter until onions are transparent. Add ⅛ cup chopped dill to the rice along with the onions and butter. Add salt and pepper to taste.

Pick young, fresh beet leaves, wilt them in a hot sun or hot oven at 200 degrees for a few minutes. Place a tsp. of rice on each beet leaf, fold sides over filling and roll bottom to top. Place in layers in a casserole dish. Pour ½ cup cream over the holubtsi, cover and bake in oven at 300°F for ½ to ¾ of an hour.

BEET LEAF DOUGH HOLUBTSI

Bread Dough:

2 pkgs. yeast
½ cup warm water
1 tsp. sugar
2 cups scalded milk
4 cups warm water
¼ cup melted butter

8 cups flour
3 eggs beaten
2 tbsp. salt
1 tbsp. sugar
6½ cups flour

Dissolve 1 tsp. of sugar in ½ cup water, sprinkle with yeast and let stand for 10 minutes.

To the milk water liquid add the melted butter, dissolved yeast, and 8 cups of flour. Let rise in a warm place until double in bulk, about 1 hour. Now add the salt, beaten eggs, sugar, and remaining flour. Knead well until dough is smooth and falls away from hands. Place in a greased bowl and brush the top with melted butter or oil. Place in a warm place and let rise until double in bulk, it will take about 2 hours. Punch down. When dough has risen to double in bulk, place a piece of dough, the size of a walnut, on a beet leaf, and roll up. Place holubtsi loosely in a pot to allow for dough to rise to double in bulk again. Arrange in layers, dotting each layer with butter, cover tightly, bake in a moderate oven of 350 degrees for ¾ to 1 hour. Serve with dill sauce.

HOLUBTSI CABBAGE ROLLS

1 head sweet or sour cabbage
1 tbsp. butter or cooking oil
¼ tsp. pepper

1 tbsp. salt
1 small onion
1 cup rice

Take head of cabbage, cut out core from centre, place cabbage into a container and pour boiling water over it. Cover and after a few minutes, remove the softened leaves. Take each separate leaf and cut off the thick vein.

Wash the rice thoroughly. Place in a 2 quart casserole. Half fill with water and cook about 30 minutes, stirring constantly. Saute butter or oil add onions. Add to the rice. Season. Mix well. Place a teaspoon or more of mixture onto each cabbage leaf and roll in a way so the rice will not fall out. Place each Holubtsi side by side in a pot. Cover with boiling water and oil, tomato soup and cream and oil are nice. Pour enough liquid to cover the rolls. Bake till a fork twisted in the roll breaks the roll in half.

SAUERKRAUT AND SPARE RIBS

2 lbs. spareribs   1 medium onion, diced   salt to taste
1 clove garlic   1 quart sauerkraut

Wash and cut spareribs into serving size. Cover with water, bring to a boil and skim. Simmer for ½ hour, add 1 quart sauerkraut, plus a quart of water, onion, and garlic. Cook until spareribs are done. Serve.

BAKED MACARONI AND CHEESE

2 cups medium sauce   **White Sauce:**
1½ cups grated cheese   2 cups milk
½ cup dry bread crumbs   4 tbsp. flour
1¼ cup macaroni, elbow   2 tbsp. butter
    or spaghetti   1 tsp. salt

Cook macaroni in 1 quart boiling water, to which two teaspoons salt was added. Drain. Arrange in layers: macaroni, sauce, and cheese. Cover with bread crumbs. Bake in moderate oven, 350 degrees F. for 20 to 30 minutes.

PERFECT ROAST CHICKEN

Roast at 400 degrees for 1 hour and 10 minutes. Makes 8 servings.

2 whole broiler fryers; about 3 to 3½ pounds each
½ cup or 1 stick margarine or butter, softened
6 cloves garlic, minced
1 tsp. salt
¼ tsp. pepper
¼ cup peanut oil

Rinse chicken inside and out. Pat dry with paper towelling.

Combine ¼ cup of the butter, garlic, salt, and pepper in a small mincing bowl. Rub chickens, inside and out, with the garlic butter mixture. Close vents with skewers or thread until the legs are together.

Heat remaining ¼ cup butter with oil, in a small saucepan, until the butter is melted. Brush chickens with part of this mixture. Place chickens on their sides on a rack in a roasting pan.

Roast in a hot oven (400 degrees) for 25 minutes. Remove from oven; turn chickens on reverse side. Brush well with butter-oil mixture, and return to oven for another 25 minutes. Remove from oven. Place chickens on their backs and brush with remaining butter and oil and continue roasting another 20 minutes, or until fork tender. Remove from oven and allow to rest for 15 minutes before carving.

LLOYD'S POTATO PANCAKES

½ cup flour
1 tsp. salt
1 tsp. baking powder
¼ tsp. pepper
1 tbsp. grated onion

1 egg
½ cup milk
2 tbsp. butter, melted
1¾ cups grated raw potato
1 clove of garlic

Sift dry ingredients together. Add milk, egg, melted butter, grated potatoes, and onion. Stir. Drop by spoonfuls onto greased hot griddle. Fry until golden brown on each side. Serve with apple sauce and bacon or ham; with cottage cheese and sour cream.

A blender can also be used to mix ingredients together.

CABBAGE AND RICE CASSEROLE

1 medium sized cabbage, shredded
1 lb. finely ground beef
½ lb. ground pork
1 lb. rice

1 tin tomatoes
salt to taste
4 tbsp. butter or shortening
3 med. sized onion, chopped

Saute the onion in butter until slightly brown. In a casserole mix both kinds of meat, add seasoning and mix again.

Wash rice, cover with water and cook for 10 minutes. Combine rice with meat mixture. Add cabbage and tomatoes. Mix and bake at 325°F for 45 minutes.

PORK CHOPS OR SPARERIBS IN TOMATO SAUCE

3 lbs. spareribs or pork chops   1 can tomato soup

Wash and cut spareribs in serving pieces. Place in casserole. Sprinkle with salt and pepper. Slice 1 medium onion. Pour 1 can tomato soup over and bake for 1½ hour at 350 degrees, or until done. Last ½ hour, add potatoes and carrots. A nice dish, all in one.

CHEESE ROLLS (NALYSNYKY)

6 eggs
½ cup warm water
1 tsp. sugar
½ tsp. salt

1 cup milk
1½ cups flour
cottage cheese

Mix eggs, water, salt, sugar and beat well. Add milk and flour, beating to a smooth batter. Grease skillet and fry cakes real thin, roll pan around to cover bottom of pan. Brown just one side. Remove cake on a warm plate. Continue frying till all batter is used. Then spread with cottage cheese, a little salt and sugar added to cheese. Roll cakes up like jelly roll. Cut in 1½ - 2" pieces. Place in greased casserole and pour sweet cream over rolls to cover. Bake in moderate oven 30 - 45 minutes. Serve.

YEAR ROUND FRIED CHICKEN II

Prepare raw chicken for frying.
Shake in bag:

1 cup flour	1 tbsp. paprika
2 tsp. salt	½ tsp. poultry seasoning
½ tsp. pepper	¼ tsp. garlic salt

Fry in hot oil until both sides are golden color. Put lid on saucepan and simmer. Place in oven for 30 minutes at 350°F.

TWO MINUTE LIVER SLIVER

Cut ½ lb. beef, calf, or lamb liver into slivers
Combine in a plate:

1 tbsp. corn starch
¼ tsp. thyme, salt and pepper to taste   ½ tsp. paprika

Roll liver in starch mixture. Melt a few spoonfuls of salad oil or butter in a fry pan. Add the liver and stir over medium heat for 2-3 minutes. Add parsley to taste and serve.

PORK AND MUSHROOM CASSEROLE

Mushrooms are used in meat dishes in a variety of ways. They are not a luxury in Ukraine, but almost an everyday staple.

3 thin slices bacon, chopped	seasoned flour
1 cup sliced mushrooms	salt and pepper
1 small onion, chopped	¼ cup sour cream
1 pound sliced pork tenderloin	½ cup canned mushroom liquid

Pan fry the bacon until crisp and remove it to a separate bowl. Brown the mushrooms and onions in the bacon fat. Combine with bacon. Dip the meat in the seasoned flour and brown it in the remaining fat. Arrange the meat in a baking dish, alternating it with a mixture of the bacon, mushrooms and onion. Sprinkle with pepper and salt. Combine liquid with sour cream, season to taste and pour over the layers. Cover and bake in moderate oven 350°F. for about 45 min.

LIVER AND VEGETABLE CASSEROLE

1 lb. baby beef liver	1 small carrot, diced
seasoned flour	½ green pepper, diced
1 medium onion, chopped	½ tsp. salt and pepper
½ cup diced celery	1 cup tomatoes or tomato soup

Cut liver into small pieces. Toss in seasoned flour and brown in fat. Place in casserole, add vegetables, seasonings, and pour over tomatoes. Cover and cook 350°F. for 40 min.

JIFFY TURKEY CASSEROLE

3½ cup tomatoes
2¼ cup tomato juice
¼ cup oil
¼ cup onion (chopped)
3 cups diced cooked turkey
¼ cup green pepper

1 tsp. salt
1 tsp. garlic powder or 1 clove, chopped
Dash of cayenne
1 cup peas, carrots or any vegetable
¼ cup sliced stuffed olives

In a large saucepan, combine tomatoes, tomato juice, oil, onion, green pepper and seasoning. Stir in rice. Bring to a boil, add vegetables, turkey and olives. Pour into a large casserole. Cover and bake in a moderate oven, 350°F., for 1 hour and 25 minutes.

PORK HOCKS OR SPARERIBS AND SAUERKRAUT

This is a very tasty and inexpensive dish.

3-5 lbs. spareribs or 4 pork hocks
1 tsp. salt
1 medium onion, chopped
1 cup water

1 qt. sauerkraut
¼ tsp. pepper
1 clove garlic, chopped fine

Cut ribs or pork hocks into serving pieces. Place meat in a large casserole, add salt, onion, garlic, pepper, sauerkraut, and water. Cover and simmer for about 1½ hours or until tender. Taste the kraut for acidity if too strong, rinse it in warm water, before adding it to meat. Serve with mashed or baked potatoes.

MEAT LOAF

2 lbs. ground beef, lean
⅔ cup dry bread crumbs or
    dry bread soaked in water
1 small onion
1 egg, beaten

¼ cup green pepper
½ cup water
½ cup rolled oats
salt and pepper to taste
1 can tomato soup

Mix everything together. Put in a loaf pan or casserole. Pour 1 can of tomato soup over and bake until done. 45-60 min at 350 degrees.

BUCKWHEAT CASSEROLE

1 cup buckwheat grits
3 tbsp. shortening or lard
½ cup onion, diced
3 cups boiling water

¾ lb. garlic sausage
¼ tsp. pepper
1 tsp. salt

Pick grits over, rinse well with warm water. Fry onion in lard until limp. Slice sausage and fry about 10 min. Add to mixture, mix well. Pour into casserole. Add seasoning and bake 1 hour in 350 degree oven.

Bacon and onion are nice or any other meat can be used.

BEEF STEW

1 lb. stewing beef
3 tbsp. flour
1 clove garlic
salt and pepper to taste
1 medium onion

3 carrots
1 turnip, diced
¼ cup celery, optional
1 cup shredded cabbage
1 potato (medium) diced

Cut meat into cubes. Dredge in flour and brown in hot oil. Add chopped onion and garlic, salt and pepper. Stir until the onion is a golden colour. Add enough water to cover meat. Bring to a boil. Simmer gently or bake in a moderate oven. 300°F for 1½ - 2 hours. Add vegetables about ½ hour before stew is ready.

MEAT BALLS

1 lb. ground beef
2 tbsp. minced onion
½ cup bread crumbs
1 egg, beaten

1 tsp. salt
¼ tsp. pepper
¼ cup water
1 clove garlic, minced

Combine ingredients together, mix well. Shape into balls about 2-3 inches in diameter. Brown meatballs slowly. Nice with a can of cream of mushroom soup poured over the meatballs and baked for 1 hour at 325°F.

1. NACHYNKA CORNMEAL CASSEROLE

1 cup cornmeal
3 tbsps. sugar
½ quart milk
½ tsp. salt

2 tbsp. chopped fine onions
½ cup butter
3 eggs, plus ½ cup cream

¼ cup roasted chicken drippings or 1 tbsp. chicken in the mug.

Scald the milk, then add the finely chopped onion, fried in butter. Slowly add the cornmeal, stirring to prevent lumps. Slowly add milk until mixture thickens.

Beat eggs and add ½ cup cream. Add this to the cornmeal. Add chicken drippings or soup base. Mix well. Bake uncovered in an oven for ½ hour at 350°F

2. NACHINKA

1 cup cornmeal
4 cups water
4 tsp. chicken soup base
3 slices bacon, chopped,
   fried with 1 large onion

Dash of salt
2 tsp. sugar
1 tsp. parsley

Heat corn meal in oven for 15 minutes, at 300°F. Cut bacon in cubes and fry. When bacon is done crisp, add chopped onions and fry until onions change color. Combine cornmeal, bacon with onions. Stir well. Add seasoning. Mix boiling water with chicken base. Pour over corn meal and mix well. Bake at 350°F. for 30 minutes.

3. NACHINKA

¾ cup butter
1 small onion, grated
1 lb. cornmeal (2 cups)
2 tbsp. chicken in the mug

6 eggs beaten
3 cups milk (heated) or more
½ cup sugar

Melt butter in Dutch oven, add onions and fry slowly not to brown. Add cornmeal and heat thoroughly, stirring constantly to avoid burning. Add enough milk and stir mixture till it forms thick paste. Add sugar and more milk as it cooks. Stir thoroughly to avoid lumps, add more milk. The mixture is quite thick now. Beat eggs, add slowly and mix thoroughly. The Dutch oven should be full. Bake about 2 hours in 350°F. oven. Serve.

NALYSNYKY (ROLLED PANCAKES)

4 eggs
1 cup flour

1 cup milk
½ tsp. salt

Beat eggs until light. Add milk and remaining ingredients. Beat until smooth. Butter fryng pan lightly and heat pan over moderate heat. Pour a few tablespoons of the batter in the pan, just enough to give it a thin coating. Tilt the pan back and forth to spread batter evenly.

When lightly browned on the bottom, remove the cakes to a warm plate. Cook only on one side. Butter pan lightly each time.

Spread cakes with cottage cheese filling. Place the browned side on the outside in rolling.

Cottage Cheese Filling:

salt and sugar to taste   2 cups cottage cheese   2 egg yolks

Mash cheese and egg yolks, add chopped dill or green onion. Spread this on cakes roll and put them in a casserole. Dot with butter or add cream. Bake 20 min. at 350°F

BUCKWHEAT FILLING FOR CABBAGE ROLLS

2 cups med. coarse buckwheat
5 tbsps. butter or fat
½ lb. cubed bacon

2 tsp. salt
5 cups boiling water or
  soup stock
1 med. onion

Pick over the buckwheat and put in a shallow pan. Dry in 350 degree oven stirring frequently until kernels are very dry. Fry the onions in butter, add to the buckwheat along with the boiling water or soup stock salt and fat. Bring to a brisk boil until surface water is absorbed. Season to taste. Cover and bake in 350° oven for about 20 minutes. Cool before using for Pyrezhky, cabbage or beet leaves.

TASTY SPARERIBS

Wash and cut 4 lbs. spareribs in desired size. Arrange in a baking dish, season with salt and pepper. Pour 1 can of tomato soup over. Add chopped onions. Bake till done at 350°F.

Vegetables can be added the last ½ hour of baking.

KEN'S BARBECUED SPARERIBS WITH GARLIC

4 lbs. spareribs
4 cloves garlic, minced
1 large onion, diced
1 cup ketchup
2 tsp. salt
¼ cup butter

dash of cayenne pepper
2 tsp. dry mustard
½ cup vinegar
¼ cup brown sugar
⅓ cup molasses

Wash and cut spareribs into serving portions. Put in a large skillet with boiling water and salt. Boil 15-20 minutes. Meantime get the sauce ready.

Fry onion in ¼ cup butter, add ketchup, salt, garlic, mustard, molasses, cayenne, ¼ c. vinegar, ¼ cup brown sugar. Take the ribs out and put into a shallow casserole. Pour the sauce over.

Cover and bake in a moderate oven for 1 hour at 350°F turning ribs over half ways through cooking time.

BAKED BUCKWHEAT (KASHA)

Kasha is a cereal cooked like porridge or baked and used in a variety of ways.

2 cups buckwheat grits
½ tsp. salt
1 tsp. butter
5 cups water

½ lb. bacon, diced, fry til brown
1 medium onion, chopped
⅛ tsp. pepper

Pick over grits, rinse well, until water is clear. Combine buckwheat with water, salt and butter. Boil 15 minutes. Then put the pot in a 350°F oven. Bake for 30 minutes, lower to 300°F and bake 30 minutes more.

Kasha may be served with scalded milk as a cereal, or served with a sauce, fried diced bacon and onions are nice or with bread crumbs browned in butter. If you add bacon and onions you could bake as a casserole — ¾ - 1 hour at 350°F.

Kasha, Ham and Mushroom Casserole

Kasha goes well with a number of foods. Here is a nice way of using it. Arrange in a casserole, alternate layers of baked buckwheat kasha, chopped ham and cooked mushrooms.

Top with a layer of kasha. Sprinkle last layer with one of the following: soup stock, mushroom stock, meat drippings, or water. Cover and bake for 30 minutes in a 350°F. oven.

Serve with any favorite preparation of cabbage or sauerkraut.

PORK CHOPS COUNTRY STYLE

3 whole carrots
4 pork chops, 1 inch thick
seasoning to taste

4 medium potatoes
4 medium onions
½ cup water

Dredge chops in flour and season. Brown on both sides in melted fat. Arrange vegetables in casserole. Season. Add chops and ½ cup water. Cover and bake at 350°F for 1 hour.

BAKED MEATBALLS IN MUSHROOM GRAVY

1 lb. chuck beef, ground
½ lb. shoulder pork, ground
1 medium onion, minced
½ cup uncooked white rice
1¼ tsp. salt
¼ tsp. pepper
1 cup soft bread crumbs or
   cracker crumbs

1 egg, beaten
1 clove garlic, crushed
1 cup hot milk
1 can condensed cream of
   mushroom soup
1 cup milk or water

Mix the first nine ingredients and shape into round balls. Place in a 2 quart casserole. Mix the soup and other ingredients and pour over the meat balls. Cover and bake in a moderate oven, 350 degrees for 1¼ hours. Serve 6.

BARBECUED SAUSAGES

2 lb. pork sausages

Boil in water for 10 minutes and prick to let out all the fat.

½ cup onion, chopped
2 cups ketchup
¼ tsp. pepper
4 tsp. sugar
1 tsp. dry mustard
1 tsp. celery salt or ½ cup
   chopped celery

¾ cup water
4 tbsp. vinegar
¼ cup chopped green pepper
½ tsp. tabasco sauce
1 tsp. worcestershire sauce

Add sausages to all this and bake at 350 degrees for 45 min. Serve with plain cooked rice or noodles.

MACARONI AND WIENERS

2 cups uncooked elbow macaroni
2 tbsp. margarine
½ cup green pepper, diced
1 small onion
2 tbsp. flour
1½ cups milk

1-10 oz. can celery soup
½ lb. wieners, sliced
1 tsp. prepared mustard
½ tsp. salt
1 cup shredded cheese
½ cup buttered crumbs

Cook macaroni in boiling, salted water until tender and drain. Melt margarine in a skillet; add green pepper and onion. Stir, fry until tender then remove from heat and stir in the flour. Add milk gradually and return to heat. Cook until thickened, then add all ingredients except crumbs. Toss sauce with the macaroni and taste for seasoning. Spread in a 1½ qt. greased casserole and sprinkle with crumbs. Bake at 350°F 35 min. or until bubbly. Serves 6-8.

JELLIED PIGS FEET (STUDENETZ)

2 pigs feet, cut lengthwise
1 pork hock
celery stalk

1 tbsp. salt
2 cloves garlic

Scrape, trim and wash very thoroughly. Place the meat, celery, salt and garlic in a large kettle, cover with cold water and bring to a boil. Then turn heat down and simmer very slowly. Rapid boiling will make the broth milky. Cook until bones fall apart. Takes 3-4 hours. Turn heat off, add crushed garlic, cool. Remove all bones, cut up meat, arrange in a dish. Season with salt and pepper. Strain juice over meat. Chill until firm. Serve.

CHILE CON CARNE

1½ lb. lean ground beef
2 tbsp. vegetable oil
½ cup chopped onion
1 can pork and beans
1 can tomato soup

salt and pepper to taste
2 cloves garlic
⅛ tsp. cayenne
1 can red kidney beans

Brown meat in oil, add onions. Mix well. Add other ingredients and bring to a boil. Simmer for 30 - 45 min. This is delicious and freezes well.

KYSHKA (BUCKWHEAT SAUSAGES)

2 lbs. spareribs or neck bones
4 quarts water
2 whole onions
2 bouillon cubes
salt and pepper

1 bay leaf
2 lbs. whole buckwheat
2 lb. fresh pork fat
2 cups fresh blood
6 beef casings

Boil 2 lbs. pork bones or spareribs in 4 qt. water. Add 2 whole onions, salt and pepper. Boil till meat parts from the bones. When done, remove the bones and add bouillon cubes.

Dry 2 lbs. whole buckwheat in an oven, 300°F, for about ¾ of an hour. Dice 2 lbs. fresh pork fat or grind in a grinder and fry until golden brown. Add buckwheat to crackling and fat. Mix well. Add 2 cups fresh blood. Mix well, over low heat until thick. Takes 10 minutes. Pour boiling, strained, pork stock over the buckwheat. Bring to a boil, simmer 5 minutes.

Rinse casings in warm water, tie one end and fill loosely with buckwheat mixture. The buckwheat should be of pouring consistency.

Place boiling water in a shallow pan or roaster. Put 2 tin foil pie plates, upside down on the bottom of the roaster. Lay the kyshka on top on the plates or racks. Prick in several places with a needle, and boil uncovered for 25 minutes. Remove carefully, cool and store.

To warm Kyshka, put in a container, add ½ cup warm water. Place in a moderate oven, brush with crisco and heat 25 minutes at 275°F.

Kyshka may be sliced in 1½ inch pieces, heat in oil in a frying pan. Serve hot.

CRUNCHY FRIED CHICKEN

Have fowl cleaned and prepared, cut in pieces of suitable size for serving. Place in saucepan, cover with rapidly boiling water and add a peeled onion, 1 tbsp. salt, cover closely and simmer gently until tender. Allow the cooked chicken to cool in its liquid then drain thoroughly.

Dip in batter:

1 cup sifted flour	1 egg
1½ tsp. salt	¾ cup milk
½ tsp. pepper	oil for frying

Make a batter, sift flour, salt and pepper. Beat egg, add milk and gradually add to the sifted ingredients. Beat batter until it is quite smooth. Dip each piece in above batter and fry in hot oil about 20 minutes, or until golden and tender. Remove to cookie sheet, place in a moderate oven 350°F. Continue cooking until chicken is tender.

BROILED CHICKEN III

Wash and cut in pieces suitable for serving. Use Shake and Bake and put in a large plastic bag. Drop pieces of fowl, shake, put under a broiler and broil for 1 hour or until done.

CHICKEN IN CREAM, UKRAINIAN STYLE

1 young chicken	1½ tsp. salt
3 cups medium cream (sweet)	½ tsp. pepper
¼ cup flour	1 onion, chopped

Select a young chicken and wash in slightly salted water. Cut in small pieces. Arrange in a casserole. Sprinkle with salt and pepper, dust flour, repeat. Pour cream over. Add onions and bake 1 hour, till done.

SPICY BLADE POT ROAST

3 pounds shoulder blade pot roast	
salt, pepper and dry mustard	
1 tsp. worcestershire	¼ cup lemon juice
1 tbsp. grated onion	¼ cup catsup
vegetable oil	flour

Rub meat well with salt, pepper and mustard. Mix next four ingredients and 1 tbsp. oil. Pour over the meat and marinate in refrigerator over night. Next day, remove meat from sauce, dredge with flour and brown on all sides in small amount of oil in kettle or Dutch oven. Cool slightly, add sauce and bake in pre-heated oven, 325°F, 2 hours, or until meat is tender. Makes 5 or 6 servings.

ROAST LEG OF PORK WITH APPLE, LEMON AND PARSLEY STUFFING

Preparation time: 30 min.

Roasting time: 5 hours

Makes: 20 servings

12 lb. fresh leg of pork	1 large onion, finely chopped
¼ cup butter	3 apples, peeled and diced
1 cup fine dry bread crumbs	2 lbs. brown sugar
Finely grated peel of 1 lemon	1 tsp. salt
½ tsp. sage	¼ tsp. basil
1 cup finely chopped parsley	

Preheat oven to 325°F. Remove large bone from leg of pork. Prepare stuffing by cooking onion in butter in a large frying pan. When onion is soft, stir in apple, bread crumbs, sugar, peel and seasonings. Remove from heat and add parsley. The mixture will be quite dry. Place leg, fat side down, on a piece of waxed paper, spread with stuffing. Skewer and tie closed, with string.

Place in a roasting pan. Add about half a cup of water. Cover loosely and roast in preheated oven, about 25 minutes per pound.

A 12 pound roast will take 5 hours for the meat to reach an internal temperature of 170°F. Uncover the last hour and baste often.

Remove from oven and let rest for 15 minutes before slicing.

HERB FRIED CHICKEN

3 lb. frying chicken	1 tsp. poultry dressing
evaporated milk for dipping	1 tsp. sage
½ cup fine dry bread crumbs	1 tsp. paprika
½ cup flour	¼ tsp. garlic powder
1 tsp. salt	½ tsp. thyme

Cut chicken into serving pieces, wash and dry on paper towel. Mix bread crumbs, flour, salt, and seasoning. Dip chicken in milk, then in seasoned breadcrumbs. Fry in crisco until nicely browned. Drain on paper towels, then arrange in roaster. Bake, slightly uncovered at 350 degrees for 1 hour or until done.

SWISS STEAK

2 lbs. round chuck meat	1 sliced onion
1 tsp. salt	⅓ cup flour
2 cups boiling water or 1 cup water	1 clove garlic, crushed
and 1 cup tomato juice	⅛ tsp. pepper

Wipe meat, place on board, dredge with flour and seasoning. Pound flour into meat using wooden masher or edge of heavy plate. Heat heavy pan very hot, put in fat. Brown meat on both sides. Add onions, boiling water and tomato soup may be used. Cover tightly, cook below boiling. 250°F. for 2 hours.

SWISS STEAK

Take a slice of meat, about 1'' to 2'' thick, lay it on a chopping board. Sprinkle with flour and with the edge of a blunt knife, pound the meat well. Turn it on the other side and do the same, sprinkle flour from time to time. Season with salt and pepper. Put a little dripping into the frying pan. Make it hot and brown the meat nicely on both sides. Prepare some sliced vegetables such as carrots, turnips or potatoes and onions. Place those vegetables in a casserole or a granite dish, add salt and enough water to barely cover. Lay the browned meat on the top of the vegetables, put on a tightly fitting cover and bake in a moderate oven for 2½ hours.

NOTE: This is an excellent dish for wash day as the meat and the vegetables can be cooked in the same dish.

KEN'S FRIED CHICKEN LIVERS

Heat butter and ¾ cup minced onion, fry lightly and quickly.

6 fresh medium sized mushrooms, sliced thick	salt and pepper to taste ½ tsp. parsley, chopped
7 chicken livers	¼ cup Harvey's
dash of garlic salt	Shooting Sherry

Cook on high heat. Toss lightly. Add sherry at the end of cooking.

PEPPER STEAK

1 lb. chuck or round steak, cubed
1 clove garlic, chopped if desired
¼ cup cooking oil, brown above in the oil or broil.

Simmer 45 minutes, add:

1 cup green pepper, chopped
1 cup onions, chopped
½ cup celery, chopped

Simmer this 10 minutes. Add 1 tbsp. soya sauce, 1 tbsp. salt, ¼ cup water. Simmer 10 min. Blend 1 tbsp. corn starch in 1 cup water. Add to above mixture 2 chopped tomatoes and simmer 5 min. Serve pepper steak with rice. Yields 2 - 3 servings.

CHILI CON CARNE

2 lbs. ground beef	1 clove garlic
salt and pepper	1 medium onion, chopped
1 can tomato soup	1 can kidney beans
1 can pork and beans	dash of cayenne pepper

Brown ground beef in Dutch oven till no red meat is showing, add chopped onion, garlic, salt, pepper, beans and tomato soup. Cook about ½ to ¾ hours. Serve with mashed potatoes.

ROAST OF BEEF WITH ONION GRAVY

4-6 lb. rump roast
2 cups water
½ cup onion, sliced
2 tsp. worcestershire

½ tsp. marjoram
1 clove garlic
¼ cup flour
1 bay leaf

Combine water, onions, worcestershire, bay leaf, marjoram and garlic in a large heavy bottomed saucepan. Bring to a boil. Add meat. Cover, reduce heat and simmer for 3 - 3½ hours or until beef is tender. Turn meat several times during the cooking.

Remove meat and prepare gravy by blending flour, with a half cup of water to form a thin paste. Whisk into hot onion broth and stir until thickened and smooth.

BEEF ROAST

2 large onions
½ cup cooking oil
4-6 lbs. blade or cross cut rib roast
⅓ cup brown sugar
1 tsp. garlic of 4 garlic cloves, crushed

½ cup or 12 oz. bottle beer
2¼ cup tomato juice
1½ tsp. salt
½ tsp. sage
¾ tsp. basil

Thickly slice onion. Heat oil in a large saucepan. Don't skimp on the oil. Add onions and cook until soft. Meanwhile coat the beef with flour, salt and seasoning. Save remaining flour mixture. Remove onions when soft. Increase heat to medium high and brown meat well on all sides. Reduce heat to medium. Blend the remaining flour mixture in the hot oil. Stir in beer. Whisk in tomato juice. Add sugar and garlic and stir until thickened, return meat and onion to pan. Cover, reduce heat and simmer for 3 - 3½ hours or until roast is done.

(SHARON'S) LASAGNA

Sauce:
1½ lbs. ground beef
2 cups onions, diced
2-8 oz. cans tomato sauce
2 tsp. salt
¼ tsp. basil crushed
1 tbsp. parsley flakes
1 tbsp. sweet pepper flakes

2 cloves garlic minced
½ lb. ground pork
2 tbsp. olive oil
1 cup water
1 tsp. pepper
3 tbsp. sugar
1 tbsp. celery flakes
1 can mushrooms

Saute onions and garlic in hot oil till brown. Remove and add meat, brown well. Drain fat from pan. Return onion and garlic, add tomato sauce, water, sugar and flakes and seasoning. In mixing bowl combine 1 pint cottage cheese, ½ cup grated parmesan cheese, 1 tbsp. parsley flakes, ½ tsp. salt, ½ tsp. crushed oregano, 1 lb. mozzerella cheese, (thinly sliced) ½ cup grated cheese, 10 oz. pkg. Lasagna noodles (cooked and cooled).

Combine 15 ingredients alternate layers of noodles, cottage cheese, mix meat sauce, mozzerella and ½ cup parmesan cheese and bake about 1 hour or until done.

SWEET AND SOUR SPARERIBS

Wash and cut 3½ lbs. spareribs into serving pieces. Drain well. Shake ribs in flour in paper bag and broil or deep fry till they are light gold in color. Put in large skillet.

Sauce:

1 cup brown sugar	½ cup vinegar
1 cup chicken broth or 1 cup water and 1 tbsp. chicken in the mug.	5 tbsp. corn starch in ½ cup water
	3 tsp. soya sauce
Bring to a boil and mix:	3 tsp. cooking oil

Bring to a boil and pour over spareribs. Mix and put in the oven, preheated to 350°F. Bring to a boil, turn heat down and simmer for ½ hour. Serve with fried rice.

SARDINES WITH SAUERKRAUT

2 cups raw sauerkraut, taste for acidity, if too strong, rinse
2 cans sardines
¼ cup onion, chopped
2 tbsp. cooking oil
salt to taste

Mix together and serve.

BAKED MACARONI AND WIENERS

2 cups cooked elbow macaroni
1 lb. wieners, cut in ½ - 1 inch pieces
1 can tomato soup
1 medium onion
6 slices of bacon

Combine macaroni, wiener, onion and tomato soup in a casserole. Put strips of bacon on top and bake 1 hour at 325 degrees.

MACARONI AND CHEESE LOAF

3 tbsp. drippings (bacon)	1½ cups stale bread or crumbs
2 onion, chopped fine	½ tsp. pepper
2 cloves garlic, crushed	2 tsp. salt
1½ lbs. ground pork or beef	2 cups elbow macaroni cooked
¼ lb. smoked ham, minced	4-6 oz. of cheese, diced
2 cups milk	3 eggs beaten

Heat drippings and add onions and garlic, fry onion until clear or soft. Add next 4 ingredients. Beat until blended. Then add crumbs and seasoning. Stir in macaroni eggs and cheese. Press into large loaf or two smaller pans. Bake at 350°F. for 1½ hours or until done. Cool and chill or serve hot.

⑤⑤⑤⑤⑤⑤⑤⑤⑤ Fish ⑤⑤⑤⑤⑤⑤⑤⑤⑤

SALMON PATTIES

1 can red salmon
2 eggs

1 cup crushed cracker crumbs
½ cup milk
1 small onion, minced

Combine ingredients. From into patties and fry in a little oil on both sides. Serve.

BAKED FISH (PECHENA RYBA)

Saute 1 cup each grated carrots, celery, chopped onion, 1 clove crushed garlic, and 1 bay leaf in 3 tbsp. oil until tender. Add 1½ cups canned tomatoes. Simmer 5 minutes. Add ½ cup tomato juice. Puree. Salt and pepper to taste. Brush with oil 2 lb. sole or flounder fillets. Sprinkle with lemon juice, salt and pepper and arrange fillets in oiled baking dish. Top with pureed vegetables. Bake at 375 degrees for 20 minutes. Garnish with parsley. Serves 8 to 10.

FISH FILLETS IN WINE

2 lbs. fish
3 tbsp. butter
½ cup dry white wine
⅓ cup water

1 egg yolk, beaten
salt and pepper
1½ tbsp. butter
1½ tbsp. flour
juice of 1 lemon

Cut fish into serving pieces. Sprinkle with salt and pepper and let stand for ½ hour. Put water, wine, butter, and lemon juice into a pan large enough to hold the fish in a single layer. Bring to a boil and simmer gently for about 15 to 20 minutes. Remove fish to a platter and keep hot. Make a smooth paste of melted butter and flour. Stir in wine until sauce thickens. Spoon egg yolk into sauce, then mix the rest of sauce. Season to taste. Pour sauce over fish and serve.

POACHED SALMON

Boil 3 potatoes till just cooked. Slice 1 medium onion, add 2 salmon steaks and a little parsley. Cook another 8 to 10 minutes, to poach.

JELLIED FISH

3 lb. raw fish
3 cups water
1 small onion, diced

2½ tsp. salt
⅛ tsp. pepper
1 pkg. unflavored gelatin

Clean and wash fish thoroughly in cold water. Cut into serving pieces and place into sauce pan. Add water and bring to a boil. Add onion and salt. Simmer slowly for 1 hour. Lift the fish out carefully into a platter. Strain juice. Soak gelatin in 1 tbsp. cold water. Add to the juice and stir well. Now pour juice over fish and let set at least 6 to 12 hours.

BAKED STUFFED FISH

3 lbs. fish, cleaned
½ cup onion, diced
½ cup celery, diced
1 can mushrooms, drained
½ cup butter

2 tbsp. parsley, chopped
2 cups bread crumbs, soft
2 tbsp. water
salt and pepper
1 clove garlic, minced

Prepare stuffing by cooking onion in butter. Add other ingredients to butter. Simmer for 10 minutes. Stuff inside fish cavity. Cover fish with tin foil. Place in oven at 350°F for 40 minutes or until fish comes off in flakes when tested with a fork.

TUNA NOODLE LOAF

3 eggs, beaten
1 cup milk
1 cup grated cheese
2 cups cooked noodles

1 green pepper (chopped)
2 tsp. onion, minced
2 tbsp. butter
salt and pepper to taste
1 can tuna

Combine eggs and remaining ingredients except tuna. Grease casserole and arrange drained tuna in bottom of pan. Arrange noodles over tuna and bake in 350 degree oven for 30 to 35 minutes. This is delicious served with tomato sauce or cheese sauce.

SALMON CAKES

2 cups water or milk
½ cup yellow corn meal
1 tsp. chopped onion
1 tsp. salt
⅛ tsp. pepper

1 can — 1 lb. salmon
1 egg
¼ cup flour
fat for frying

Combine water and salt in sauce pan, bring to boiling and add corn meal gradually, stirring constantly. Cook until mixture thickens, stirring often. Cover, cook over low heat 10 minutes, remove from heat and cool. Drain salmon, flake, removing any skin and small bones. Add salmon, onion, egg and pepper to cornmeal mixture and chill mixture for 2 hours, or until firm enough to handle easily. Shape into 8 medium size cakes. Dust with flour. Melt enough fat to cover bottom of pan, fry cakes 5 minutes on each side or until done. Serve with chili sauce and lemon wedges.

FRIED PICKEREL

2 pickerel fillets, about 1¼ lbs.
¼ cup mayonnaise or salad dressing
3 tbsp. butter or margarine
3 tbsp. onion, chopped
vinegar

salt and pepper to taste
1 tbsp. olives chopped
1 tbsp. parsley, chopped
2 tsp. tarragon

Cut fillets in half, sprinkle with salt and pepper. Melt butter or margarine in large fryer. Add chopped onion and fish. Fry fillets 4 minutes on each side or until tender. Combine remaining ingredients, spread over fish. Heat through, basting with drippings! Place on pre-heated platter. Garnish with parsley and stuffed olives. Serves 4.

HOT CRAB SOUFFLE

8 slices of bread
½ cup mayonnaise
1 green pepper, chopped
1 onion, chopped
1 cup celery, chopped

2 cups crab meat or shrimp
3 cups milk
4 beaten eggs
1 can mushroom soup
grated cheese and paprika

Dice 4 slices of bread into a greased baking dish, mix crab meat, onion, green pepper, celery and mayonnaise, spread over the diced bread. Trim crusts from the other 4 slices of bread and place over the crab mixture. Mix together the eggs and milk, pour over the ingredients in the dish. Bake in the oven at 325°F for 15 minutes. Spoon the soup over all and sprinkle the top with grated cheese and paprika. Bake for 1 hour more. Serve immediately.

CLAM CHOWDER

½ cup bacon, chopped
¼ cup chopped onion
1 cup diced raw potatoes
1 cup diced raw carrots
¾ cup diced raw celery

salt and pepper
1 bay leaf
1 sprig thyme
1-15 oz. can minced clams

Fry bacon, add onion and fry lightly. Add salt and pepper, water, carrots, celery, potatoes, bay leaf and thyme and let simmer 20 minutes. Add clams and liquid and let simmer another 15 minutes.

TUNA MACARONI SALAD

7 oz. can tuna, drained and flaked
1 cup chopped celery
½ cup chopped sweet pickle
3 cups cooked shell macaroni

½ cup mayonnaise
3 tbsp. French Dressing
1½ tsp. salt
½ tsp. pepper

Mix together mayonnaise, French Dressing, salt and pepper. Toss in rest of ingredients, mix lightly. Spoon in mound shapes on to chilled plates. Makes 6-8 servings.

SALMON ROLL

2 cups flour
4 tsp. baking powder
½ tsp. salt
4 tbsp. oil or shortening
2 eggs, beaten

½ cup milk
1½ cups salmon (1 tin)
4 tbsp. milk
2 tbsp. lemon juice
3 tbsp. onions, diced
1½ to 2 tbsp. parsley (chopped)

Sift together first 3 ingredients. Add shortening or oil and mix well. Add milk to eggs to measure ¾ cup. Add to first mixture. Roll out on floured board in sheets 8 inches long and about ¼ inch thick. Combine remaining ingredients, spread on dough and roll like jelly roll. Bake in preheated oven of 425°F about 30 minutes. Serve with egg sauce or cheese sauce.

Egg Sauce

To 2 cups medium white sauce, add 2 hard cooked eggs, diced, and 2 tbsp. diced parsley.

SALMON LOAF

1 cup cooked salmon
1 cup breaded crumbs, soaked
   in 1 cup scalded milk
1 tsp. salt
1 tbsp. shortening or oil

1 tsp. onion, diced
2 egg yolks, beaten
1½ tsp. lemon juice
2 egg whites, beaten; folded
   in last

Mix in order given. Bake in well greased and covered pan.

LOBSTER

10-12 lobster tails or 2 lobsters
1 bay leaf
1 quart water
1 tsp. salt
1 teaspoon pepper

½ tsp. thyme
½ tsp. marjoram
1 tsp. celery salt

Place water in a large skillet. Add all ingredients and bring water to a boil. Add 10-12 lobster tails or 2 lobsters can be cooked at one time. Cover. Cook over medium heat about 20 minutes. Remove from pan. Serve at once with melted butter and garlic salt. To serve lobster tails, split in half lengthwise. 1 lobster tail serves 1 person.

PICKLED HERRING

Brine:

2 cups water
1 tbsp. whole spices
   tied in a cloth bag
2½ cups vinegar
Boil the above 10 minutes·
   then cool
sliced onion

Soak herring at least 24 hours, change water if too salty. Clean and cut herring in 1 inch pieces. Put in sealers with layer of onion. Pour cooled brine over herring and seal. Let stand about 4-5 days before it will be ready to eat.

SALMON LOAF II

1 large can of salmon
2 cups bread crumbs
½ cup milk

2 tbsp. melted butter
2 eggs, beaten
salt and pepper to taste

Cheese Sauce

2 tbsp. butter
2 tbsp. flour

½ cup grated cheese
¼ tsp. salt
1 cup milk

Put drained salmon in bowl. Remove bones, if any. Add bread crumbs, milk, salmon juice, butter, eggs, and seasoning. Mix well. Pour in casserole and bake at 350 degrees for 40 to 50 minutes.

Cheese sauce: In a double boiler, melt butter and add flour. Add salt; stir often. Add milk and cook for a few minutes. Add cheese. Stir until cheese is well blended. Serve on salmon loaf.

NACHYNENA RYBA (STUFFED FISH)

5 lb. salmon
1 med. onion, chopped
1 cup celery, finely chopped
¼ cup oil
2 cups dry bread cubes

⅛ tsp. salt
⅛ tsp. pepper
¼ tsp. poultry seasoning
¼ tsp. sage
¼ cup water

Scale and clean the fish. Cook onion and celery in oil. Combine all the remaining ingredients. Stuff the salmon and brush outer surface with oil. Bake on large cookie sheet at 400 degrees allowing 10 minutes for every inch of fish thickness. Serve on hot platter garnished with lemon wedges and parsley.

SALMON LOAF

1 cup flaked cooked salmon
1 cup stale bread crumbs, soaked in
   1 cup scalded milk
2 egg yolks, beaten
1 tsp. salt

1 tbsp. butter
1½ tsp. onion chopped fine
1 tsp. lemon juice
2 stiffly beaten egg whites,
   folded in last
1 clove garlic smashed (optional)

Mix in order given. Bake in well greased pan at 350°F until done.

WHOLE BAKED HADDOCK

Wash and clean thoroughly, a 3 lb. haddock. Put in a fish poacher.
Pour:

1-28 oz. can of tomatoes
½ cup celery, chopped
½ cup onion, chopped
pinch of thyme

1 bay leaf
pinch of tumeric
¼ cup parsley

Bake at fairly high heat, 450°F, allowing 10 minutes per inch of thickness.

SALMON ROLL

2 cups flour
4 teaspoons baking powder
½ tsp. salt

4 tbsp. shortening or butter
1 egg
½ cup milk

Sift the first three ingredients, add shortening and mix well with fork. Beat egg and to it add milk to make ¾ cup. Add to flour mixture. Make soft dough. Roll out on floured board, making square approximately 8x8 inches and ¼ inch thick. Spread dough with following mixture:

1 tin salmon, 1½ cups
4 tbsp. milk
2 tbsp. lemon juice

2 tsp. finely chopped onion
1 tbsp. chopped parsley

Roll same as jelly roll. Bake in a hot oven 425 for 30 minutes. Cut in ½ inch slices. Serve with medium sauce to which 1 or 2 hard boiled eggs have been added.

HERRING AND MUSHROOMS IN SAUCE

In some regions of Ukraine this dish is included in the menu of the traditional Christmas Eve supper, but the cream is omitted and the butter is replaced with oil.

1 salt herring
1 tbsp. grated onion
2 tbsp. butter or cooking oil
2 cups sliced mushrooms

1 tbsp. butter or oil
1 cup water or vegetable stock
3 tbsp. sour cream
2 tbsp. flour

Prepare the herring by soaking it for 24 hours. Change the water a few times. Clean the herrings, skin them, and remove the bones. Soak fillets in the milk to cover, for 1 or 2 hours. Drain, pat dry and cut herring into 1 inch pieces. Cook the onion in butter until tender. Add the mushrooms and cook, stirring frequently, for about 5 minutes. In another pan, brown the flour lightly in the butter or oil. Add the water or vegetable stock gradually, stirring constantly, until the sauce boils. Stir in the cream, mushrooms and herring. Simmer for 10 minutes to blend the flavors. Serve with sauerkraut, varenyky or buckwheat holubtsi.

FISH FILLETS IN WINE

2 pounds fillets of any whitefish
salt and pepper
2 tbsp. butter
⅔ cup dry white wine
¼ cup water

Juice of 1 lemon
1 tbsp. flour
1 tbsp. butter
1 egg yolk
salt and pepper

Cut fish fillets into serving pieces. Sprinkle with salt and pepper and allow to stand for 30 minutes. Put the butter, wine, water and lemon juice into a pan large enough to hold all the pieces of fish in a single layer. Arrange the fish in the pan. Bring to a boil and then lower the temperature. Cover and simmer gently for 15 minutes. Remove the fish to a hot platter and keep hot. Make a smooth paste of the flour and melted butter. Stir in the wine stock, gradually. Cook until the sauce thickens. Spoon some sauce into the beaten egg yolk and mix with the rest of the sauce. Season to taste. Strain the sauce and pour over the fish.

OYSTER CREAMEY ON TOAST

1 pint oysters
1½ cups milk
½ cup cream
lemon juice to taste

salt and pepper
⅓ cup butter
⅓ cup flour

Heat oysters until the edges curl. Strain off the liquid. Heat the milk. Heat the oyster liquid and skim. Melt butter, sift in the flour, stir and cook together. Add hot milk and oyster juice all at once, whisking until it is smooth and thick. Add the cream to the oysters and season. Serve on hot buttered toast.

FISH WITH GARLIC SAUCE

Serves four.
Sauce:
1 large potato
1 teaspoon salt
½ cup olive oil
¼ cup water

4 cloves garlic, crushed
1 cup finely ground almond
¼ cup vinegar
Lemon juice, see recipe.

4 steaks of cod, haddock or halibut, about 4-6 oz. each, salt and pepper, all purpose flour for coating, oil for deep frying.

To make garlic sauce: peel and quarter the potato and cook in lightly salted water until tender. Drain and set aside. Add crushed garlic and salt. Stir in almonds and potatoes, continue pounding until a smooth paste forms. Add olive oil very gradually beating well after each addition. Stir in the vinegar and water and mix thoroughly. The mixture should be the consistency of thick mayonnaise. If necessary add lemon juice until the correct consistency is achieved. Wipe the fish with a damp cloth or absorbent paper. Sprinkle with salt and pepper to taste and coat the pieces with flour. Deep fry in hot oil until crisp and golden brown. Drain on absorbent paper. Serve hot with garlic sauce.

NOTE: When less garlic is used, this is an excellent sauce to accompany vegetables.

PICKLED PERCH

Clean and cut into 1 to 1½ inch pieces.

Soak in salt no less than 24 hours.

Rinse fish in cold water. Drain. Bring 1 quart vinegar to a boil. Put fish in boiling vinegar until redness in backbone disappears; about 5 to 8 minutes. Lift fish out and drain. Then make a brine of 1¾ quarts vinegar and ¾ quart water. Bring to a boil. Cool and pour over fish that is put into quarts. Put a tsp. of oil and sliced onions into each quart. This should be ready to eat in three days.

DELICIOUS PAN FRIED FISH

2½ to 3 lbs. fish
½ cup flour
1 egg, slightly beaten

2 tbsp. milk
butter or oil
salt and pepper

Rinse fish with cool water and cut into serving pieces. Sprinkle with salt and let stand 30 minutes. Coat each piece with flour; dip in the beaten eggs and milk then in flour again. Pan fry in hot oil or butter until brown on each side. Mince 2 cloves of garlic in 2 tbsp. water. Sprinkle over fish and let simmer for 15 minutes. Serve.

HERRING IN CREAM

6 to 7 herrings
1 cup cream
1 tbsp. mustard
6 tbsp. gherkins, finely chop

2 tbsp. cooling oil
3 herring milts
3 hard cooked egg yolks
1 tbsp. vinegar or lemon juice
3 tbsp. onion, minced

Sauce:

Cream together yolk of eggs, milts, and oil. Add the other ingredients (except herring) and mix well.

The herring should be soaked in water 24 to 36 hours. Change water if too salty. Remove the skins. Fillet the herring, taking care to remove the bones. Make a roll or put in flat layers. Let stand 3 days before serving.

▣▣▣ Breads and Buns ▣▣▣

WHITE BREAD

3 pkgs. yeast
1 qt. scalded milk (lukewarm)
1 cup butter or margarine
1 cup sugar
4 eggs

1 qt. water
2 tsp. salt
1 lemon, juice and rind
flour

Soak the yeast as directed on package, using part of the lukewarm water. Scald milk, add butter and sugar. Add beaten eggs, balance of lukewarm water, salt, rind and juice and blend. Add the yeast and mix well. Add 5 cups of flour, beat until smooth and light, and let the batter rise in a warm place until bubbles appear (about ½ hour).

Add and knead in about 12 cups flour, or more, for a medium soft dough. Knead thoroughly until the dough is smooth and falls way from hands. Cover and let rise until double in bulk. Knead down and let rise as before. This amount of dough will make 6 to 8 loaves of bread.

Grease the pans. Form the dough in loaves and let rise until double in bulk. Brush top with beaten eggs. Bake in oven at 350 degrees for ½ hour; then lower heat to 325 degrees and bake for one hour or until done.

WHITE BREAD

1 tsp. sugar
⅛ cup sugar
¼ cup lukewarm water
1 tbsp. salt

1 pkg. dry granular yeast
3 tbsp. melted shortening
4 cups boiled water, cooled to lukewarm
flour

Soften the yeast in lukewarm water as directed on the package. To boiling water, add shortening, salt, and sugar. Cool. Combine the softened yeast, salt, sugar, shortening, and 6 cups of the flour. Beat until smooth. Cover and set in a warm place to rise. The dough is ready when it is light and bubbly. Add small amount flour and knead until the dough no longer sticks to hands. Turn it out on a floured board and knead until smooth and satiny. Return dough to a bowl, cover, and set aside in a warm place to rise until double in bulk. Knead. Let rise for about ½ to ¾ of an hour. Cut the dough into three portions. Shape them into loaves. Place each loaf into a well-greased loaf pan. Cover and let rise in a warm place until more than double its original size. Bake in a moderate oven of 375°F for about 45-60 minutes. Remove loaves from the pans and cool on a wire rack.

HEALTH BREAD

2 pkgs. yeast	⅔ cup oil or shortening
1 tsp. sugar	1 cup cornmeal
1 cup lukewarm water	1 cup wheat germ
4 cups milk scalded	1 cup oatmeal
3 beaten eggs	1 cup hulled sunflower seeds
⅓ cup honey	2 cups dark rye flour
⅓ cup molasses	4 cups whole wheat flour
2 tbsp. salt	2 cups all purpose flour

Dissolve 1 tsp. sugar in the one cup of warm water in large bowl. Sprinkle yeast and let stand for 10 minutes. In the meantime, get your other ingredients ready. Add salt, honey, molasses, and shortening or oil to your milk. Check temperature of this mixture, should be lukewarm. Now add your beaten eggs and mix into the large bowl with yeast. Stir with wooden spoon very thoroughly. Now start adding dry ingredients starting with cornmeal and mixing after each addition. Now work in flour and knead. This dough takes about 15 minutes of kneading until no longer sticky. Cover and place in warm place to rise for 2 hours or until double in bulk. Punch down and let rest for ½ hour. Now divide dough into four pieces. Place shaped loaves in four standard buttered loaf pans and let rise to double in size. Bake at 400 degrees for 15 minutes, then reduce heat to 350 for 45 minutes longer until crust is dark gold or sounds hollow when tapped on bottom of loaf.

WHOLE WHEAT BREAD

12 cups whole wheat flour	5-6 cups scalded milk or water
½ cup honey or brown sugar	½ cup melted shortening
2 packages dry yeast	or cooking oil
1½ tbsp. salt	⅓ cup molasses

Dissolve the 1 tbsp. sugar in ½ cup warm water, add yeast. Let stand 10 minutes. Cool milk to lukewarm and mix ingredients. Knead until smooth and elastic. Cover and allow to rise until double in bulk. Shape the dough into loaves and place into greased loaf pans. Let rise until double. Bake in 375°F oven for 40-60 minutes. Tap the bottom of the bread. If it sounds hollow it is completely baked. Cool the loaves on racks.

AIR BUNS

2 pkgs. dry yeast	2 tsp. sugar
1 cup warm water	

Put the above ingredients together in a bowl, let stand for 10 minutes.

18 cups flour	1 cup lard
1½ tsps. salt	1 cup sugar
2 tbsp. vinegar	6 cups water

Mix together. Let rise in warm place until double in size. Punch dough and allow to rise again, until double. Make into buns. Let rise in warm place for 2½ hours. Bake in 350°F for 25-30 minutes.

WHOLE WHEAT BANANA BREAD

1 cup mashed ripe bananas
  (about 4 medium)
2 eggs, beaten
½ cup shortening, melted
1 cup whole wheat flour

¾ cup flour
¾ cup sugar
1 tsp. baking powder
¾ tsp. salt
½ tsp. baking soda

Mix well bananas, eggs, and shortening, set aside. In large bowl mix well, flour, sugar, baking powder, salt and soda. Stir in banana mixture just to blend. Spread in greased loaf pan. Bake in 350°F oven for 1 hour or until toothpick inserted comes out clean.

FOUR FRUIT BREAD

¾ cup dried apricots cut up
½ cup chopped dates
1 cup orange juice
¼ cup salad oil
1 cup flour (all purpose)
½ cup brown sugar
2 tsp. baking powder

1 cup seedless raisins
1 tbsp. orange rind
½ cup chopped nuts
1 egg
½ tsp. salt
1 cup whole wheat flour

Soak apricots in hot water for 1 hour. Sift the dry ingredients. Prepare orange rind, nuts and fruit. Beat the egg together with orange juice and salad oil. Combine fruit mixture to the dry ingredients. Stir well.
Bake at 350 degrees for 1 hour.

CHRISTMAS CARROT LOAF

1½ cups chopped cherries
1½ cups glazed fruit
1½ cups currants
1¼ cups cooking oil
2 tsp. baking soda soaked in 1 tsp. water
2 tsp. baking powder
5 cups flour

1 can frozen concentrated orange juice
3 cups grated carrots
2 cups brown sugar
7 eggs
½ tsp. salt
1 tsp. vanilla

Mix currants, glazed fruit and cherries then add frozen orange juice and leave to soak overnight. Next morning add the 3 cups carrots and let stand.
Mix the sugar and 7 eggs and beat until very fluffy. Then add the oil, soda, salt, baking powder, vanilla and flour. Mix well and then add to the fruit mixture.
This batter must be very stiff. Spoon into loaf pan lined with oiled paper and bake for 1½ hours at 350 degrees.

BREAD, BUNS, PYRIK AND PYREZKY (WITH VARIOUS FILLINGS)

3 pkgs. yeast
½ cup warm water
1 tsp. sugar
2 cups scalded milk
½ cup melted shortening
  or butter
4 cups warm water

3 eggs beaten
8 cups flour
1½ tsp. salt
¼ cup sugar
6½ cups flour

Dissolve 1 tsp. of sugar in ½ cup water, sprinkle with yeast, let stand for 10 minutes.

To 8 cups of flour add milk, water, melted butter, dissolved yeast mix and let rise in warm place until double in bulk, about 1 hour. Now add salt, sugar, beaten eggs and remaining flour. Knead well until dough is smooth and no longer sticks to the hand. Cover and keep in warm place and let rise until double in bulk.

Punch down. Let dough rise for at least an hour again. Place on a bread board and divide into 6 equal portions. This will make 3 braided loaves of bread or pyrik with cabbage and cottage cheese filling or a pan of buns and pyrezhky with any of the following fillings.

Chop fine 1 medium, head of fresh cabbage, add 1 tsp. of salt, mix and let stand for 30 minutes. Then remove juice by squeezing thoroughly.

Fry one medium finely chopped onion in 3 tbsp. oil or butter until golden in color and add the cabbage. Fry on low heat for 4-6 minutes, add a few drops of lemon juice. Add 1 cup of dry cottage cheese and mix well.

Cottage Cheese and Dill Filling:

1 cup dry cottage cheese
1 tbsp. butter
2 tbsps. dill weed

1 egg yolk (beaten)

Mix together and fill.

SWEET DOUGH FOR BUNS OR BAKED CHEESE DUMPLINGS

½ cup water dissolved in
  2 pkgs. yeast
1½ cups lukewarm milk
½ cup butter or shortening
½ cup sugar

1 tsp. salt
3 eggs
6 cups flour

Combine ingredients together, knead and let rise in warm place, till double in size. Make into buns or baked cheese dumplings. Bake at 375°F for 20-25 minutes.

OVERNIGHT BUNS

In a small bowl put 1 tsp. sugar, 1 cup lukewarm water, 2 pkgs. of yeast and let rise. Add 2 cups cold water, ½ cup oil, ¾ cup sugar, 2 tsps. salt, and 8 cups flour to the above.

Mix and let rise, punch down and let rise again. Make into buns and let rise overnight and bake in morning in oven at 375 degrees for about 12 minutes.

HOT CROSS BUNS

1 pkg. yeast	1 tsp. salt
¼ cup lukewarm water	¼ cup butter (melted)
1 cup scalded milk	½ tsp. nutmeg
½ cup sugar	½ tsp. cinnamon
1 cup currants (washed well)	2 eggs beaten
	3¼ cups all purpose flour

Soften yeast in lukewarm water. Scald milk and add sugar, salt and butter. Cool milk to lukewarm and add 1 cup flour and spices. Beat well. Add softened yeast and eggs, beat well. Add remaining flour to make a thick batter. Beat thoroughly until smooth. Cover and let rise until doubled in bulk. Punch down, add currants let rise again. Drop by spoonfuls into greased muffin pans filling half full. Let rise until double in size. Bake in moderate oven 375°F for 20 minutes. Once they're out of the oven, mix confectioners sugar with a little hot water and ½ tsp. vanilla and mark a cross on each bun.

CINNAMON TOAST

2 servings.

1 tbsp. sugar	2 tsp. margarine
¼ tsp. cinnamon	2 slices bread

Mix sugar and cinnamon.
Toast the bread and butter it on one side.
Sprinkle the sugar mixture over the buttered side of the toast.
Cut in attractive pieces and serve on hot bread plates.

FRENCH TOAST

8 slices of bread	1 tbsp. sugar
4 eggs	pinch of salt
1 cup milk	2 tbsp. butter or margarine
2 tbsp. Grand Marnier	confectioners sugar

Beat eggs, milk, Grand Marnier, sugar and salt. Dip slices of bread turning to coat evenly.

In hot butter in skillet, saute bread until golden on each side. Sprinkle each with confectioners sugar.

Makes 4 servings.

DATE AND NUT LOAF

1 cup sugar
1 cup butter
1 egg, well beaten
4 cups flour
4 tsp. baking powder

2 cups sweet milk
1 cup walnuts
1 cup chopped dates
pinch of salt

Make batter as for cake. Let rise for 20 minutes.
Bake in slow oven for 1½ hour. Makes 2 loaves.

DATE LOAF

1 cup dates (cut into a bowl, pour 1 cup boiling water and 1 tsp. soda).
Let cool while you proceed with other ingredients.

½ cup butter
1 cup brown sugar
1 egg

1 tsp. baking powder
2 cups flour
½ cup walnuts

Combine the above ingredients then fold in cooled dates.
Bake in a loaf pan about 1 hour at 325°F.

PRUNE LOAF

1 cup cooked prunes
2 cups sifted all purpose flour
3½ tsp. baking powder
½ tsp. baking soda
½ tsp. salt
½ cup brown sugar

1 cup whole wheat flour
¼ cup shortening or butter
2 tbsp. grated orange rind
1 cup milk
2 eggs, well beaten
2 tbsp. orange juice

Wash prunes, cover with water and cook until soft. (10-15 min.). Remove pits,
chop prunes or put in blender. Sift together baking powder, soda, salt and sugar.
Add flour. Put in shortening or butter, add chopped prunes and orange rind. Mix
together well beaten eggs and milk. Add to flour mixture and stir lightly.
Bake in loaf pan 1 hour at 350°F.

CARROT LOAF

4 eggs well beaten
2 cups brown sugar
1½ cups Mazola oil
3 cups grated raw carrots
2 tsps. baking powder
1½ tsp. cinnamon
1 tsp. cloves

2 tsps. vanilla
3 cups flour
1 cup raisins
1 cup walnuts
2 tsps. baking soda
½ cup cherries (optional)

Mix the above ingredients in order given.
Bake in two loaf pans for 1¾ hours at 300°F.

BRAN AND DRIED FRUIT LOAVES

½ cup molasses
½ cup butter or margarine
1 cup whole bran cereal
1 cup wheat germ
½ cup yellow cornmeal
½ cup raisins or chopped, dried
  apple slices

1 tsp. salt
2 cups boiling water
1 envelope dry yeast
2 eggs
3 cups whole wheat flour
3 cups white flour

Mix molasses, butter, cereal wheat germ, cornmeal, raisins, salt and water. Cool to warm, stirring occasionally. Stir in yeast until dissolved. Beat in eggs and cups whole wheat flour. Gradually stir in just enough flour to stiffen dough. Turn out on lightly floured surface. Knead until smooth. Place in greased bowl, cover, let rise in warm place until double. 1½-2 hours. Punch down. Let rise for ½ hour. Divide in half, shape each in smooth loaves. Cover, let rise in warm place until double, about 45 minutes.
Bake at 375°F for 40-45 minutes until loaf sounds hollow when thumped. Let cool. Remove from pans.

CINNAMON LOAF

Mix 4 tbsps. brown sugar with 1½ tsp. cinnamon and set aside.

¼ cup butter
2 eggs
2 cups flour
½ tsp. soda
2 tsps. vanilla

1 cup brown sugar
1 cup sour milk
1 tsp. baking powder
½ tsp. salt

Cream butter and sugar, add beaten eggs. Mix dry ingredients, and add to butter mixture, alternately with sour milk. Put half the batter into a loaf pan. Sprinkle remainder of cinnamon mixture on top. Pour remaining batter on top. Swirl with a knife.
Bake 50-60 minutes at 350°F.

Cakes and Tortes

APPLESAUCE CAKE

1¾ cups sifted flour
1 tsp. baking soda
¼ tsp. salt
½ tsp. cloves
½ cup shortening or margarine
1½ tsp. cinnamon

1 cup brown sugar
1 egg beaten
1 cup thick applesauce
1 cup walnuts

Combine dry ingredients. Dredge raisins and walnuts with a little flour. Cream shortening, sugar, and add the egg. Add dry ingredients alternately with applesauce, shortening, and finishing with dry ingredients. Add raisins and nuts, mix just enough to blend. Bake in 350°F in a lined greased loaf pan, 50-60 minutes. This cake tastes better the next day.

APPLE TORTE

1½ cups all purpose flour
1 tsp. baking soda
1 tsp. cinnamon
¼ tsp. salt
½ cup butter

1 cup sugar
1 egg beaten.
½ cup cold coffee
2 cups finely chopped apples
1 tsp. vanilla

Sift flour, soda, cinnamon and salt three times. Cream butter, and sugar. Add eggs and vanilla. Mix flour a little at a time, with coffee. Add the chopped apples.
Pour into well greased pan 9 x 13 x 2. For topping mix:
   ½ cup sugar, ½ cup coconut, ½ cup walnuts, ½ tsp. cinnamon. Sprinkle over the top of cake and bake in 350°F oven for 45-50 min.

RAW APPLE CAKE

1 cup shortening
1½ cups sugar (white)
¾ cup brown sugar
3 eggs
1 cup buttermilk
1 tsp. vanilla
1 cup coconut

2½ cups flour
1 tsp. soda
1 tsp. baking powder
2 tsp. cinnamon
1 tsp. salt
2 cups diced apples
1 pkg. chocolate chips

Cream shortening, brown sugar and white sugar, add eggs and buttermilk, sift flour, soda, baking powder, cinnamon and salt together and add to egg mixture. Add vanilla. Sift a small amount flour over apple, and stir into batter and blend well. Pour into greased 9 x 12 inch pan. Combine remaining ingredients.
Bake for 50 minutes in a 350°F oven.

APPLESAUCE CAKE WITH CARAMEL FROSTING

1 cup shortening
2½ cups applesauce
2 cups white sugar
1 tsp. each cinnamon, allspice
    cloves and salt

3 cups flour
3 tsp. baking soda
2 eggs beaten
½ cup margarine
1 cup brown sugar
¼ cup milk
1¾ - 2 cups sifted
    confectioners sugar

Melt shortening in suacepan, add applesauce, white sugar, and spices and heat thoroughly. Stir in flour and soda. Stir in eggs. Pour into greased 9 x 12 inch pan. Bake 40 minutes at 350 degrees or until done. Melt margarine in saucepan, add brown sugar and boil over low heat for 2 minutes stirring constantly. Add milk and continue stirring until mixture comes to a boil. Remove from heat and cool. Add confectioners sugar and gradually, beating well after each addition until of spreading consistency. Spread over cake.

1 cup washed raisins could be added to batter if desired.

BOILED RAISIN CAKE

To 2 cups washed raisins, add about 2 cups water and boil raisins until tender. Set to cool.

3 cups flour
2 tsp. baking soda
1 tsp. cloves
2 tsps. cinnamon
1 cup walnuts chopped
1 cup raisin water

1 tsp. allspice
2 tsp. nutmeg
½ cup butter
1 cup sugar
2 eggs beaten

Sift dry ingredients. Cream butter, sugar, add eggs, and raisin water, then dry ingredients. Mix well and add walnuts and raisins. Bake until done, in a 9 x 12 greased pan at 350°F.

BANANA CAKE

½ cup butter
1 cup sugar
2 eggs, well beaten
1 tsp. soda dissolved in
    4 tsp. boiling water

2 cups flour
2 tsp. baking powder
pinch of salt
1 cup mashed bananas
1 cup nuts chopped

Cream butter, sugar, add beaten eggs and mix well. Dissolve soda in boiling water and add to mashed bananas.

Sift dry ingredients together, add alternately with mashed bananas to first mixture. Add nuts.

Bake in 350°F oven until done.

BANANA CAKE

1½ cups white or whole wheat flour
¾ cup brown sugar
¾ tsp. baking powder
¾ tsp. baking soda
½ tsp. salt
½ cup walnuts (chopped)

¼ cup buttermilk
¼ cup shortening
2 egg yolks
2 egg whites
1 tsp. vanilla
¾ cup mashed bananas

Sift flour, baking powder, soda and salt. Add creamed sugar and shortening, ¼ cup buttermilk and vanilla and egg yolk. Beat hard for 1 minute. Beat egg white until soft peaks form. Fold into flour mixture along with nuts. Bake at 350°F for 35-40 minutes.

CARROT CAKE

2 tsp. baking powder
1 tsp. cinnamon
3 cups flour
2 tsp. baking soda
1 tsp. salt
1 cup cooking oil
2 cups sugar
4 eggs

1 cup chopped, mixed
    candied fruit
3 cups grated carrots
1 cup raisins
1 cup chopped nuts

Sift dry ingredients together, set aside. Combine oil, sugar, add eggs one at a time. Beat well after each addition until light and fluffy. Gradually add dry ingredients. Add grated carrots and fruit. Mix well.

Bake in greased 9 x 12 inch pan. Bake at 350 degrees for 1½ hrs. until cake tests done.

FROSTING FOR CARROT CAKE

1 pkg. 8 oz. Philadelphia cream cheese
1 lb. icing sugar sifted
1 tsp. vanilla or lemon juice

Cream cheese then add icing sugar and lemon juice.
Ice cake after it has cooled thoroughly.

CARROT MUFFINS

1½ cups flour
1 cup sugar
1 tsp. cinnamon
1 tsp. baking powder
1 tsp. vanilla
½ cup crushed pineapple or
    applesauce

1 tsp. soda
½ tsp. salt
¾ cups oil
2 eggs beaten
1 cup grated carrots

Sift dry ingredients into a large bowl, make a well shape in centre and add oil, eggs, grated carrots, pineapple and vanilla. Beat well till smooth. fill baking cups ⅔ full. Bake 20-25 min. at 350°F.

COFFEE CAKE

¾ cup shortening
1 cup sugar
2½ cups all purpose flour
2 tsp. instant coffee
½ tsp. baking soda
1¼ tsp. baking powder

¾ tsp. allspice
1 tsp. cinnamon
½ tsp. salt
½ cup current jelly
3 eggs
¾ cup buttermilk

Beat eggs well, add sugar, salt, shortening and beat for 1½ minutes. Sift together flour, baking soda, baking powder, cinnamon, allspice, instant coffee and add to creamed mixture. Mix well. Blend current jelly. Pour into 2 round cake pans, grease and bake at 350°F for 35 minutes.

CRANBERRY CARROT CAKE

3 cups sifted all purpose flour
2 tsp. baking powder
1 tsp. baking soda
1 tsp. cinnamon
¾ tsp. nutmeg
½ tsp. salt
½ tsp. cloves

1 cup whole cranberry sauce
1 cup brown sugar
1 cup white sugar
1 cup cooking oil
4 eggs well beaten
1 cup grated carrots

Sift dry ingredients together. Add to cream mixture. Blend well and pour into 2 loaf pans. Bake in 350°F oven for 1½ hrs. or until top is browned and springs back when lightly touched.

CHOCOLATE CAKE

¾ cups semi sweet chip or
    4 Baker squares
½ cup boiling water
1 cup Crisco shortening, or butter
2 cups brown sugar
4 egg yolks
1 tsp. vanilla

2½ cups flour
1 tsp. soda
½ tsp. salt
1 cup buttermilk
4 egg whites stiffly beaten

Melt chocolate in water, cool. Cream butter and sugar, light and fluffy. Add egg yolks one at a time. Add vanilla and melted chocolate. Mix well. Combine flour, soda and salt. Add alternately with buttermilk to the chocolate mixture beating until batter is smooth.

Fold in egg whites. Pour batter into 9 x 13 in. pan. Bake at 350 degrees for about 60 minutes or until cake springs back when lightly touched in centre. Cool and frost.

CREAM SPICE CAKE

1 cup brown sugar
½ cup butter
1 cup sour cream
3 eggs
2 cups flour
1 cup raisins

½ cup walnuts
1 tsp. each soda, cloves
2 tsp. cinnamon
3 tsp. allspice
½ tsp. each ginger, nutmeg

Cream together butter and sugar. Add one egg at a time, cream well. Dissolve soda in sour cream and add to creamed mixture. Sift spices, flour and salt, add raisins and nuts. Combine with creamed mixture. Bake in oven 350 - 375 until done.

COTTAGE CHEESE CAKE

2 lbs. cottage cheese (dry)
¼ lb. butter melted
6 eggs separated
2 cups sugar

2 oranges juice and rind
½ tsp. salt
1 lb. graham wafer crumbs

Mix butter, sugar and cheese, cream well. The cheese should be pressed through a fine sieve. Add orange juice, rind, well beaten egg yolks and mix until smooth and fluffy. Fold stiffly beaten egg whites into the mixture.

Roll wafers to a fine crumb. Add 2 tbsp. melted butter and mix well. Pat ½ the wafers in a long buttered pan. Spoon in the cheese mixture, then sprinkle the remainder of the crumbs on top of the cake. Bake in moderate oven 375°F or 350 until a toothpick comes out clean.

CHEESE CAKE

Crumb crust

1½ cups graham cracker crumbs
6 tbsp. melted butter

1 tsp. cinnamon
¼ cup icing sugar

Take out ½ cup of crumbs. Line dish bottom and sides with the remainder of the crumbs. Bake in a pan with removeable rim if possible. Chill crust thoroughly.

Cheese Filling

3 tbsp. flour
1 cup sugar
2 lbs. cottage cheese
  about a quart

1 tsp. lemon juice
¼ cup cream
4 egg yolks
¼ tsp. salt

Mix sugar with cream. If the cheese is dry use twice the amount of cream. Add cheese, beaten egg yolks, flour and lemon juice. Fold in egg whites (beaten). Fill crumb shell and sprinkle remaining crumbs on top. Bake in a moderate oven 350°F for one hour.

BUTTERLESS, EGGLESS, MILKLESS CAKE

Put in a saucepan and boil for three minutes.

1 cup sugar	1 tsp. cloves
1 cup water	¼ tsp. salt
1½ cups raisins	½ tsp. nutmeg
	½ cup shortening

Remove from heat and let cool then add

2 cups flour	1 tsp. soda dissolved in a little
¾ tsp. baking powder	boiling water

Bake for 45 minutes at 325°F. This cake keeps well.

SIMPLE CHERRY CAKE

2 cups sugar	1 tsp. vanilla
1 cup flour	½ cup butter
1 tsp. soda	1 can cherries, drained
	½ cup cream

Mix 1 cup sugar, flour, soda and cherries thoroughly. Bake at 350 degrees for 45 minutes. Bring remaining sugar, butter, vanilla and cream to a boil, cook until thick. Serve warm over baked cake. Yields 6 servings.

SOUR CREAM CHOCOLATE CAKE

2 cups sugar	2 cups flour
½ cup shortening	¼ tsp. salt
2 eggs	½ cup cocoa
1 cup sour cream	1 tsp. vanilla
1 tsp. soda	1 cup hot water

Cream sugar and shortening, add eggs and beat. Add soda to cream, mix in. Sift dry ingredients together. Add alternately with vanilla and hot water. Pour into greased pan.
Bake at 375 degrees for 25-30 minutes.

ORANGE CHOCOLATE CAKE

¾ cups brown sugar	juice and rind of 1 orange
¾ cup white sugar	2 cups flour
½ cup shortening (Crisco)	1 tsp. soda
2 eggs	3 squares unsweetened chocolate
1 cup buttermilk	

Cream sugar and butter, add eggs and melted chocolate, juice and rind. Dissolve soda in buttermilk, add flour. Beat well. Bake in layer or oblong pan at 350°F until done.

66

SAUERKRAUT CHOCOLATE CAKE

2¼ cups flour
½ cup cocoa
1 tsp. each soda and baking powder
¼ tsp. salt
⅔ cup butter or Crisco

1½ cups sugar
4 eggs
1 tsp. vanilla
1 cup strong coffee
⅔ cup sauerkraut rinsed
drained and put though food
chopper

Combine first 5 ingredients in large bowl, cream butter, sugar, and eggs. Add vanilla. Add liquid and dry ingredients alternately beginning and ending with flour. Stir in sauerkraut. Bake in layered pans or oblong pan at 350 degrees 25-30 minutes.

BLACK FOREST CHERRY CAKE

6 eggs
1 tsp. vanilla
1 cup plus 3 tbsp. sugar divided
½ cup sifted flour
½ cup unsweetened cocoa
10 tbsp. butter, clarrified with
milky solids poured off

¼ cup cold water
2 tbsp. plus ¼ cup Kirsch divided
3 cups heavy cream chilled
½ cup icing sugar
1 cup fresh pitted red cherries
poached in syrup or 1 cup canned
cherries rinsed drained patted dry
18 oz. bar chocolate shaved into curls

Whole fresh cherries or maraschino cherries with stems patted dry with paper towels.

Combine eggs, vanilla and one cup sugar, beat until lemon in color, about 10 minutes. Fold in dry ingredients, add 2 tbsp. butter at a time (do not over mix). Pour batter into three 8 inch layer pans. Line the bottom with buttered wax paper. Bake at 350 degrees until done about 15 minutes. Cool 5 min. Remove from pans, cool completely. Heat water and remaining 3 tbsp. sugar to a boil in 1 quart saucepan over medium heat, continue to boil 3 to 4 minutes. Stir in 2 tbsp. Kirsch, sprinkle syrup evenly over cake.

Whip cream adding icing sugar and add remaining Kirsch in thin stream, continue beating until firm peaks form. To assemble cake place one layer on serving plate, spread with ½ inch of whipped cream, ½ inch away from edge, and spoon cherries over cream. Set second layer on top of cherries, spread with ½" layer of cream as before. Top with third layer. Use remaining cream to frost sides and top of cake. Press some chocolate curls into cream on sides of cake, garnish top of cake with remaining chocolate and whole cherries.

EIGHT MINUTE CAKE

Take ½ cup milk and boil with a round tsp. of butter. Then add:

¾ cup sugar	2 eggs beat lightly
¾ cup flour	⅛ tsp. salt
1 small tsp. baking powder	½ tsp. lemon flavoring

Add milk to this mixture beating well. This is a very thin mixture but it will turn out very well. Bake in moderate oven 350 degrees for about 25 minutes.

3 LAYER POPPY SEED CAKE

¾ cup poppy seed	2 tsp. vanilla
¾ cup butter	4 egg whites
¾ cup milk	3 tsp. baking powder
1½ cups sugar	2 cups flour

Soak poppy seed in milk for 5-6 hours or overnight. Cream butter, sugar, then add vanilla, poppy seed and the milk in which the poppy seed was soaking. Add flour which has been sifted with baking powder. Mix well. Last beat egg whites and mix slightly into the batter. Pour in three layer pans, which have been greased and lined with paper. Bake in preheated 350 degrees oven for 25 minutes.

Filling for this cake:

1 cup sugar	4 egg yolks
pinch of salt	1 cup chopped walnuts
2 tbsp. cornstarch	2 cups milk
1 tsp. vanilla	

Mix sugar, cornstarch and salt. Add beaten egg yolks, then add scalded milk. Boil this until mixture begins to bubble. Remove from stove, add nuts, cool and spread between layers of cake. Frost with marshmallow frosting.

Marshmallow Frosting

Combine in saucepan:

2 cups sugar

⅔ cups water

¼ tsp. cream of tartar

Stir over low heat until sugar is dissolved. Bring to a boil and cook without stirring until syrup spins a thread. Remove from heat.

2 egg whites beaten to soft peaks. As soon as the syrup stops bubbling, pour it slowly in a thin stream into the beaten egg whites. Beat with an electric mixer while adding the syrup. Add 1 cup marshmallows cut small, and continue beating until the frosting is of spreading consistency. Then fold in 1 tsp. vanilla. This is enough frosting to cover this cake.

SPECIAL APPLE CAKE AND FROSTING

4 cups peeled and chopped apples
2 cups sugar
¾ cup chopped walnuts
¼ cup raisins
2 eggs well beaten
½ cup salad oil

2 tsp. vanilla
2 cups flour
2 tsp. soda
1½ tsp. cinnamon
dash nutmeg
1 tsp. salt

In bowl, stir together apples, sugar, walnuts, raisins, beaten eggs, salad oil and vanilla until well combined. Onto waxed paper, sift flour, soda, cinnamon, nutmeg and salt. Pour flour mixture over apple mixture and combine well. Turn batter into a greased and floured 9 x 13 x 2 inch pan. Bake in a 350 degrees oven for 45-60 minutes or until cake is done. Allow to cool before frosting.

Frosting:

8 oz. cream cheese, softened   ½ cup butter or margarine
1 lb. icing sugar (approximately) use amount to obtain spreading consistency.
Extra chopped walnuts for garnish.

In bowl cream cheese and butter together until light and fluffy. Add icing sugar, as necessary and vanilla. Blend until smooth. Spread frosting on cooled cake. Sprinkle generously with chopped walnuts for garnish.

WHOLE WHEAT SOUR CREAM COFFEE CAKE

1¾ cups whole wheat flour
1 tsp. each baking powder and soda
⅛ tsp. salt
½ cup butter or margarine softened
⅔ cup brown sugar (packed)

2 eggs
1 tsp. vanilla
1 cup sour cream
Bran nut filling recipe
    follows

Mix flour, baking powder, soda and salt and set aside. Cream butter, sugar, eggs and vanilla until light and fluffy. Stir in sour cream alternately with flour mixture until blended. Spread ⅓ of butter in greased 9 inch square pan. Sprinkle on about ½ cup filling. Repeat layering twice. Bake in preheated 350 degrees oven for 35-40 minutes or until done.

Bran nut filling:

Mix ⅓ cup packed brown sugar, ½ cup branflake cereal, ⅓ - ½ cup chopped nuts and 1 tsp. cinnamon. Makes about 1½ cups.

JELLY ROLL CAKE

1 cup flour
⅓ cup hot water
1 cup sugar
4 eggs

¼ tsp. salt
1½ tsp. baking powder
½ tsp. vanilla

Beat eggs add sugar, beat well. Then add vanilla and hot water. Sift dry ingredients together and mix. Pour in an oblong pan which has been dusted with flour. Bake for 12-15 minutes at 375°F. Place a damp cloth on a towel. Tip the jelly roll out of the pan. Spread on jam and roll tightly. Other fillings could be used such as lemon cream or cocoa pudding.

BLACK CHERRY ROLL

2 eggs
¾ cup sugar
1 cup flour
1 tsp. baking powder

¼ tsp. soda
pinch of salt
⅓ cup sour cream
½ pt. whipping cream

Line pan with waxed paper. Beat eggs until thick and add sugar. Fold dry sifted ingredients and sour cream. Bake at 400 for 12 min. Turn cake on cloth and sprinkle with icing sugar. Roll cake up when cake is cooled, unroll and fill with whipped cream. Heat 1 can of cherry filling until filling is clear and cool. Slice cake and scoop cherry filling over. Strawberries are nice instead of cherry.

LANE CAKE

½ cup butter
1 cup sugar
½ tsp. vanilla
1½ cups plus 2 tbsp. flour
1¾ tsp. baking powder

¼ tsp. salt
½ cup milk
4 egg whites stiffly beaten

Mix cake in order given. Last of all add stiffly beaten egg whites. Pour into 3 layer pans. Bake until done.

Filling

4 egg yolks
½ cup sugar
½ cup butter
½ cup walnuts chopped

½ cup coconut
½ cup cherries
3 tbsp. wine or whiskey
½ cup raisins

Cook filling in order given. Spread between layers of cake. Put favorite frosting over cake.

EASY CAKE

2 eggs beaten
1 cup brown sugar
1 cup flour
1 tsp. vanilla

½ cup milk
1 tsp. baking powder
pinch of salt
3 tbsp. butter

Boil milk and butter. Add to dry ingredients, add eggs. Bake in moderate oven for 25 minutes.

Topping

8 tbsp. brown sugar
3 tbsp. butter

4 tbsp. milk
1 cup coconut

Boil first 3 ingredients together, remove from heat and add coconut and spread on cake then put back in the oven, broil for a few minutes.

CINNAMON LOAF

Mix 3 tbsp. brown sugar with 1 tsp. cinnamon. Set aside.

¼ cup butter
2 eggs
2 cups flour
½ tsp. soda
2 tsp. vanilla

1 cup sugar
1 tbsp. cinnamon
1 tsp. baking powder
½ tsp. salt
1 cup sour milk

Cream butter and sugar, add eggs. Mix dry ingredients and add to first mixture alternately with milk. Pour into pan. Sprinkle cinnamon and brown sugar over and cut with knife. Bake at 350 for 50-60 minutes.

NURSES CAKE

1 cup crisco
2 cups sugar
3 eggs
2½ cups flour

1 tsp. cinnamon
2 tsp. soda
2 tsp. vanilla
½ tsp. salt

Combine ingredients above. Then add:

2 cups coconut
2 cups grated carrots
1 - 14 oz. tin crushed pineapple and juice
(1 cup)

1 cup walnut
1 cup cherries

Bake in 2 pans 7 x 11. Bake at 350°F for 1 hour. Freezes well. Nice as a light fruit cake.

POPPY SEED BUNDT CAKE

¼ cup poppy seed
1 cup buttermilk
¾ cup shortening or
   butter
4 eggs separted
½ tsp. vanilla
½ tsp. lemon juice

2½ cups plus 2 tbsp. flour sifted
½ tsp. soda
1 tsp. baking powder
¼ tsp. salt
1¾ cups sugar
cinnamon-sugar mixture

Soak poppy seed in buttermilk for 15 minutes. Mix shortening and sugar. Add egg yolks and flavoring. Sift flour with soda, baking powder and salt. Add this to creamed mixture alternately with poppy seed and buttermilk. Fold in stiffly beaten egg whites. Grease bundt pan well. Put in small amount of batter and sprinkle cinnamon mixture. Add more batter and repeat. Do top with butter. Bake 45 -50 minutes at 350 degrees.

COCOA CAKE (with sour cream)

3 eggs
1½ cups sugar
¼ tsp. salt
1½ cups sour cream
3 tbsp. cocoa

2 cups flour
1 tsp. baking powder
1 tsp. vanilla
1 tsp. soda

Beat eggs well, add sugar, salt and cocoa. Add soda dissolved in hot water. Sift flour and add alternately with cream. Add flavoring. Mix thoroughly and bake in 350°F oven.

LAZY DAISY OATMEAL CAKE

1¼ cups boiling water
1 cup rolled oats
1 cup shortening (crisco)
1 cup white sugar
1 cup brown sugar
1 tsp. vanilla

2 eggs
1½ cups flour
1 tsp. soda
½ tsp. salt
¾ tsp. cinnamon
¼ tsp. nutmeg

Pour boiling water over rolled oats.   Let stand until cool.   Cream shortening sugar and eggs. Add cooled rolled oats mixture. Blend in vanilla, salt. Sift flour, soda, cinnamon and nutmeg. Add to creamed mixture. Mix well. Pour batter into well greased 9 inch square pan. Bake at 350°F for 50-55 minutes. Last 10 minutes before cake is done put on this Lazy Daisy Frosting

½ cup butter or margarine
½ cup brown sugar

3 tbsp. milk or cream
⅓ cup chopped nuts
¾ cup coconut

Combine all ingredients. Spread evenly over cake. Broil until frosting becomes bubbly. Cake may be served warm or cold.

WALNUT CAKE

1½ cups brown sugar
3 eggs separated
⅞ cup milk
2¼ cups flour
½ cup crisco or butter

3 tsp. baking powder
1 cup chopped walnuts
½ tsp. salt
1 tsp. mapleine

Cream shortening and brown sugar. Add yolk of eggs. Sift flour and baking powder. Add flour and milk alternately, beating well. Add walnuts, salt and mapleine. Beat well. Add well beaten egg whites last, folding them in carefully. Bake 1 hour at 350°F.

RHUBARB CAKE

2 cups flour
½ cup butter
¼ tsp. salt

1 tsp. baking powder
1 egg (beaten)

Mix together with fork. Reserve one cupful for top. Flatten the rest into 8 x 8 inch pan.

Filling:

1½ cups sugar
¼ cup flour
4 cups chopped rhubarb

½ cup melted butter
2 eggs beaten

Sprinkle over the top the reserved first mixture, then sprinkle with sugar and cinnamon. Bake, cut in squares and serve hot or cold with ice cream or plain cream.

WHITE CHOCOLATE CAKE

⅓ lb. white chocolate
½ cup water
1 cup butter or crisco
2 cups sugar
4 eggs separated
2½ cups flour
1½ tsp. baking powder

½ tsp. salt
1 cup buttermilk
1 tsp. vanilla
1 cup chopped pecan or almonds
1 cup flaked coconut

Melt chocolate in water and cool. Beat butter and 1½ cup sugar until creamy. Add egg yolks. Stir. Sift flour, baking powder, and salt. Add to creamed mixture in thirds alternately with buttermilk, vanilla and chocolate, beat until smooth after each addition. Beat egg whites until soft peaks form. Gradually add remaining ½ cup sugar continuing to beat until stiff (but not dry). Fold into batter, then fold in pecans and coconut. Turn into three 9 inch greased pans lined with wax paper. Bake in oven 350°F about 35 minutes or until done. Frost with boiled or butter icing.

TOMATO SOUP CAKE

2 cups flour
3 tsp. baking powder
3 tsp. cinnamon
½ tsp. cloves
½ tsp. nutmeg

½ cup raisins or dates
¼ cup chopped walnuts
½ cup shortening
1 cup sugar
2 eggs
¼ tsp. baking soda
1-10 oz. can condensed tomato soup

Preheat oven to 350 degrees. Grease a 9 x 9 inch pan. Sift dry ingredients except soda. Mix fruit and nuts. In a large bowl cream sugar, shortening, add eggs beat until fluffy. Stir soda in tomato soup. Add alternately to batter with flour. Mix until smooth after each addition. Mix in raisins and nuts. Pour into pan and bake about 35 minutes. Let cool 5 minutes. Frost with caramel or cream cheese frosting.

SOUTHERN COCONUT CAKE

1½ cups flour
1 cup sugar
½ tsp. salt
½ cup shortening
1 cup milk

1 tsp. baking powder
2 eggs
1 cup coconut
1 tsp. almond flavouring

Blend everything except eggs and coconut in a bowl. Beat with electric mixer at low speed for about 2 minutes until smooth. Beat eggs, add to the batter. Fold in coconut. Bake 40-45 minutes until toothpick comes out clean.
Icing: Icing sugar, butter, milk and almond extract.

ORANGE CAKE

1 orange
1 cup raisins (washed)
1 cup sugar
1 cup sour milk
3 eggs

½ cup butter
1 tsp. soda
1 tsp. baking powder
2 cups flour
½ cup walnuts (optional)

Squeeze juice from orange and put rind, raisins through a chopper. Cream sugar and butter, add eggs. Sift flour and baking powder together. Add soda to milk and mix. Stir everything together, mix well. Bake in moderate oven till done.

Icing

1 tbsp. butter
5 tbsp. brown sugar

6 tbsp. milk

Bring to a boil and cool. Add 2 cups icing sugar and 1 tsp. vanilla. Beat until smooth.

SOUR CREAM ORANGE CAKE

1 cup sugar
½ cup butter
2 eggs
½ pt. sour cream
1 tsp. soda
1 cup ground raisins

1 medium sized orange, ground
2½ cups flour

Cream sugar and butter, beat in eggs, sour cream, soda, raisins and orange. Sift and measure flour add to batter. Turn into greased 9 inch pan (square) and bake in 350 degree oven for 35 min.

ORANGE CHIP CAKE

2 cups flour
1 tsp. ea. soda, baking
   powder
½ cup white sugar
½ cup brown sugar
½ cup shortening

1 cup sour milk
2 eggs
¼ cup grated orange rind
7 oz. semi sweet chocolate
¼ cup chopped walnuts

Sift dry ingredients together. Blend sugar and shortening. Add eggs, orange rind, vanilla, chocolate and nuts and milk. Stir well. Pour into two 9 inch greased pans lined with wax paper. Bake in moderate oven 350 degrees for 25- 30 minutes or until cake test done. Cool cake and ice.

SOUR CREAM CAKE

¾ cup butter
1½ cups sugar
3 eggs
1½ cups sour cream
1½ tsp. baking soda
1 tsp. baking powder

2¼ cups flour
filling:
½ cup brown sugar
2 tsp. cinnamon
½ cup chopped nuts

Blend first four items. Add dry ingredients. Grease oblong pan and pour some batter. Sprinkle filling then add more batter. Bake 45 minutes in 350 degrees oven.

THREE C CAKE

3 eggs beaten
½ cup milk
1 cup sugar
1 tsp. baking powder
1 tsp. baking soda
½ tsp. salt
1 tsp. cinnamon

2½ cups flour
2 cups grated carrots
½ cup cherries
¼ cup coconut
½ cup raisins
½ cup walnuts
½ cup cooking oil

Combine egg, oil, milk in bowl. Stir dry ingredients. Mix thoroughly. Stir in rest of ingredients. Turn into 4 well greased floured pans. Bake at 350°F oven for 45-50 minutes.

POPPY SEED CAKE

¾ cup poppy seed
¾ cup milk
¾ cup butter
1½ cups sugar

2 cups flour
2 tsp. baking powder
4 egg whites (beaten stiffly)
1 tsp. vanilla

Soak poppy seed in milk for 4 hours or overnight. Cream butter and add sugar then add seeds. Add dry ingredients and then the beaten egg whites. Bake in well greased layer pans at 375 degrees for 20-25 minutes.

Filling

1½ tbsp. cornstarch
1 cup milk
½ cup sugar

4 egg yolks
½ cup walnuts, chopped
1 tsp. vanilla or lemon juice

Dissolve cornstarch in a little milk and cook over low heat until milk thickens. Add sugar, beaten egg yolks and cook slowly for about 3 minutes stirring constantly. Add chopped walnuts. Cool the filling and spread between the layers of cake. Ice cake with butter icing.

POPPY FORM CAKE

1 cup shortening
1½ cup sugar
¾ cup poppy seed (soaked)
4 eggs separated
1 tsp. vanilla

1 cup sour cream
2½ cups flour
1 tsp. soda
½ tsp. salt

Cream shortening and sugar until light and fluffy. Add poppy seed. Soak in cream for 4 hours. Add yolks one at a time beating well after each addition. Stir in vanilla and sour cream. Sift together soda, flour, and salt. Add gradually to poppy seed mixture, beating well after each addition. Fold in stiffly beaten egg whites. Pour into a greased 9 or 10 inch tube. Bake at 350 degrees about 1 hour 15 minutes or until cake springs back when touched. Cool in pan and remove and frost.

BROWN SUGAR LOAF CAKE

½ cup oil
2 cups brown sugar
2 eggs
¾ cup raisins or dates
1 tsp. cinnamon
2 tsp. baking powder

½ tsp. nutmeg
½ tsp. ginger
½ tsp. soda
¼ cup hot water
½ cup milk
2 cups all purpose flour

Preheat oven to 375°F. Cream together oil, sugar, and eggs. Beat well. Add raisins and spices and mix well together. Stir in milk, sift flour, and baking powder together and beat into mixture.
Bake in 8" x 8" pan for 40-50 minutes or until done.

DARK CHOCOLATE CAKE

2 cups white sugar
⅔ cup vegetable oil

2 eggs
2 tsp. vanilla

Beat the above well for 4 minutes.

Sift:

2 ⅔ cups flour
⅔ cup cocoa
2 tsp. baking powder

1 tsp. salt
2 tsp. soda

Add alternately with 2 cups boiling water, beating well after each addition. Put in well greased 9 x 13 pan.

Bake at 325 degrees for 50 minutes.

SOUR CREAM UKRAINIAN CHOCOLATE CAKE

Cream well ⅔ cup of butter.
Measure and combine, then sift twice 1½ cups flour.

1½ cups sugar
¾ tsp. baking soda
¾ tsp. baking powder
½ tsp. salt

½ tsp. cinnamon
Combine: ¾ cup sour cream
¼ cup milk

Add liquids and dry ingredients alternately to butter, beating thoroughly after each addition.

Add 3 squares melted semi sweet chocolate
2 large unbeaten eggs
¼ cup creme de cocoa
1 cup sour cream

Beat 1 minute. Pour into 2, 9 inch round cake pans. Bake at 350 degrees for 30 minutes. Cool. Use following filling recipe between layers and on top.

Combine in heavy saucepan:

1 cup sugar
3 egg yolks

¾ cup cream
¼ cup butter

Stir over medium low heat until thick.

Add:

¼ cup coconut
1 cup chopped pecans or walnuts

1 tbsp. Creme de cocao
Cool and spread.

JELLY ROLL

6 egg yolks
½ cup boiling water
2 tsp. baking powder
1 tsp. vanilla

1 cup sugar
1½ cups flour
½ tsp. salt

Beat egg yolks until thick and lemon colored. Continue beating and adding sugar gradually until fluffy. Add ½ cup boiling water, gradually beat until fluffy. Add vanilla and add to flour mixture (flour, baking powder and salt). Grease pan and also grease wax paper. Pour into 9 x 13 inch pan. Bake at 350 degrees for 25 minutes. Sprinkle waxed paper with icing sugar. When cake is baked, immediately turn out on paper. Roll immediately without filling. Let cool, then unroll and spread with jam or jelly and roll up again.

SOUR CREAM POPPY SEED CAKE

½ cup poppy seeds
3 eggs
1½ cups sugar
1½ cups thick sour cream
1½ tsp. vanilla

2¼ cup cake flour
3 tsp. baking powder
½ tsp. baking soda
¼ tsp. salt

Pour boiling water over the poppy seeds and drain well over a fine sieve. Spread the poppy seeds over on a tea towel or brown paper and dry well. This should be done the day before baking. Beat eggs well. Add the sugar to beaten eggs. Beat in sour cream and vanilla. Sift flour with dry ingredients. Add flour to cream mixture along with poppy seeds and mix. Bake in layer pans for 35 to 40 minutes at 350 degrees.

WHOLE WHEAT SPICE CAKE

1 cup whole wheat flour
½ cup flour
1 cup sugar
1 tsp. baking soda
1 tsp. cinnamon
½ tsp. each of salt and
   nutmeg

¼ tsp. cloves
½ cup whole bran cereal
1 cup cold strong coffee
¼ cup oil
1 tbsp. vinegar
1 tsp. vanilla

Mix well flour, sugar, baking soda, spices and salt — set aside. In 8 x 8 x 2 inch baking pan mix cereal and coffee — let stand 2 minutes or until most of liquid is absorbed. Stir in oil, vinegar, and vanilla, then stir in flour mixture until smooth. Bake in 350 degrees oven for 40 minutes or until pick inserted in centre comes out clean. Cool.

RICH FRUIT CHRISTMAS CAKE

1 lb. butter
4 cups flour
½ lb. citron
1 lb. dates
½ lb. pineapple
½ cup molasses or plum
   juice
2 tsp. nutmeg
2 tsp. cloves
2 tsp. allspice

2 tsp. cinnamon
½ cup brandy or plum juice
2 tsp. soda dissolved in juice
1 lb. brown sugar
4 lbs. raisins
10 eggs
½ lb. almond
½ lb. cherries
½ lb. walnuts

Cream butter and sugar. Then add eggs well beaten, molasses, brandy and flour. Lastly add the fruit and nuts powdered with a little flour. Bake until done (3 hours) at 275°F.

FRUIT CAKE

1 lb. candied pineapple
½ lb. cherries
¼ lb. citron peel
¼ lb. orange peel
¼ lb. lemon peel

1½ lbs. bleached raisins
½ lb. currants
½ lb. pecans
½ lb. almonds blanched
½ cup brandy

Prepare all the fruit (clean and chop) cut up the nuts, soak overnight in brandy.

Next day, measure 2 tablespoons fruit juice, 1 tbsp. almond flavoring.

In a separate bowl, cream ¼ lb. butter, add 1 cup white sugar, 1 cup brown sugar. Mix well and add to beaten eggs. (6 eggs, plus 2 cups flour and ½ tsp. soda).

Sift ½ cup of measured flour over fruit and add remaining flour gradually to the creamed mixture. Mix well. Add prepared fruit and nuts. Use your hand to blend well. Pour into greased lined angle food cake pan and bake in slow oven 200 degrees for 1½ hours then raise heat to 300 degrees an bake for another 1½ hours or more. When cake is cold store in a covered crock. Sprinkle with brandy (well).

LIGHT FRUIT CAKE

1 cup butter
2 cups sugar
6 eggs
4 tsp. baking powder
2¼ cups flour
1 tin crushed pineapple
1 lb. shredded coconut

½ lb. citron peel
½ lb. blanched almonds
½ lb. red cherries
½ lb. green cherries
1 tsp. vanilla
1 tsp. almond extract
¼ cup amaretto or fruit juice

Mix and bake for 2½ hours.

CHRISTMAS CAKE

2 cups butter

2 tsp. cinnamon

1 tsp. salt

2 tbsp. pineapple juice

2 lbs. currants

½ lb. cherries

2 lbs. dates

2 cups brown sugar

2 tsp. baking powder

Grated rind and juice of 1 orange

4 cups flour

2 lbs. seedless raisins

1 lb. walnuts

7 eggs separated and beaten

Prepare cake pan. Cream together butter and sugar, add well beaten egg yolks. Sift together the flour, salt, baking powder, and spices. Mix 1 cup of this flour mixture with the fruit and nuts. Add grated rind of orange and juice to creamed mixture. Beat until light and fluffy. Add floured fruit to cream mixture. Mix well. Beat egg whites until stiff but not dry.

Fold into cake batter. Bake in 275 degrees oven 3-4 hours. Depends on the size of pan. Cool cakes. Pour some amaretto over cake and wrap well. Store in cool place.

FRUIT CAKE

1 cup butter

6 eggs

3 cups sifted flour

1 tsp. cloves

1 tsp. salt

½ cup apricot jam

1 pkg. dried apricots (2 cups)

1 pkg. assorted peel large

1½ cups brown sugar

3 tbsp. molasses

2 tsp. cinnamon

½ tsp. baking soda

1½ tsp. nutmeg

6 cups raisins rinsed well

1 pkg. assorted fruit

2 cups walnuts

Wash raisins and apricots and steam with ½ cup water for 15-20 minutes or until dry.

Beat butter and sugar. Add eggs one at a time. Blend into molasses and jam. Sift dry ingredients and add them. Add fruit and nuts. Bake at 275 degrees for 3 hours. Makes 3 loaf tins.

WHOLE NUT FRUIT CAKE

1 lb. whole pitted dates

½ lb. whole glazed red cherries

½ lb. walnut halves

½ lb. pecan halves

½ lb. whole shelled brazil nuts

1 cup chopped glazed pineapple

1 cup sifted flour

1 tsp. baking powder

⅛ tsp. salt

5 eggs

1 cup sugar

Mix and bake 1½ - 1¾ hours. Yields 2 loaf cake.

CHRISTMAS CAKE
Australian White Fruit Cake

1 lb. butter
12 eggs
1 tsp. baking powder
1 lemon, juice and grated rind
½ lb. almonds sliced
1 lb. glace cherries ½
    red and ½ green
1 lb. white sugar

4 cups flour
1 tsp. salt
½ lb. citron peel
1½ lb. white bleached sultans
4 green, 4 red, 2 yellow glace
    pineapple rings
1 pkg. apricots (precooked)

Prepare cake pans and set aside. Just fits three square wedding cake pans. Prepare fruit and let set aside. Cut cherries in half. Sift flour, baking powder and salt. Cream butter, sugar, beat in six whole eggs one at a time. Add grated rind and juice of the lemon. Separate six eggs and beat separately. Add beaten yolks to cream mixture, then add flour and fruit and last of all the stiffly beaten egg whites. Bake at 275 degrees, remembering the smaller tins will bake in a shorter time. Let cakes cool in tins, wrap well to keep moist and leave to ripen.

CINNAMON TORTE

Base
½ cup butter
½ cup sugar
4 egg yolks, beaten

6 tbsp. milk
1 cup flour
1 tsp. baking powder

Cream butter and sugar well; add well beaten eggs, milk and flour sifted with baking powder. Mix thoroughly and pour into 9 x 12 inch greased pan. Bake in a 350 degree oven for 15 minutes, or until light brown.

Filling
1 can crushed, undrained
    pineapple

2 tbsp. cornstarch
½ cup sugar

Combine and boil until thick, stirring often to prevent scorching. Cool and spread over baked base.

Topping
4 egg whites

½ tsp. cinnamon
½ cup sugar

Mix sugar and cinnamon. Beat egg whites until fairly stiff. Gradually add the sugar mixture beating constantly, until the whites hold peaks. Spread over the filling like a meringue on pie. Place in a moderate oven and bake until the top is lightly browned. Cut in long pieces 1 by 2½ inches.

BLACK FOREST TORTE

1¾ cup flour
1¾ cup sugar
1¼ cups water
1¼ tsp. soda
1 tsp. salt

1 tsp. vanilla
¼ tsp. baking powder
⅔ cup margarine, soft
4-1 oz. squares unsweetened
    chocolate, melted and cooled
3 eggs

Heat oven to 350 degrees. Brush sides and bottom of four 9 inch round layer pans with butter. Bake only two layers at a time. Measure into a large mixer bowl all ingredients except eggs. Beat at low speed to blend, beat 2 minutes at medium speed, scraping bowl frequently. Add eggs, beat two minutes more. Pour ¼ of batter in each pan; layers will be thin. Bake 15 to 18 minutes or until done. Cool slightly and remove from the pan, cool thoroughly. Alternate layers with chocolate filling on top. Do not frost sides of torte.

Chocolate Filling

1½ squares or 4 oz. German's sweet chocolate
¾ cup butter or crisco
½ cup chopped, toasted almonds

Melt chocolate bars over hot water, cool. Blend in butter and stir in almonds.

Cream Filling

2 cups whipping cream

1 tbsp. sugar
1 tsp. vanilla

Beat whipping cream with sugar and vanilla. Whip until stiff; do not overbeat.

POPPYSEED TORTE

1 cup dry ground poppy seed
8 eggs, separated
1 cup sugar

5 tbsp. flour
1 tsp. almond extract
½ cup ground walnuts (optional)

Grind poppy seed. Do not soak the poppy seed or the torte will be heavy. Beat egg yolks, adding half the sugar gradually and beating until fluffy. Add poppy seed, flour, extract, and nuts; mix well. Beat egg whites until stiff; adding the other half of the sugar. Pour the egg yolk mixture over the egg whites, folding lightly, until blended. Bake in ungreased tube pan at 350 degrees, for 45 minutes, or until done when tested.

Invert pan and cool. Ice with favorite frosting.

BLACK FOREST CHERRY TORTE

Makes 9 inch cake

1 cup all purpose flour
1 cup cornstarch
1 tsp. baking powder
3 tbsp. cocoa
5 eggs
1 cup sugar

Filling

1½ lbs. sour cherries
⅔ cup water
⅔ cup sugar
½ cup Kirsch
1 tsp. powdered gelatin
1¼ cups heavy cream
1 cup chopped almonds
1 oz. semi sweet grated chocolate

Make cake at least 24 hours before it is needed. Sift together flour, cornstarch, baking powder and cocoa. Grease a 9 inch spring form pan. Beat together eggs, sugar in a mixing bowl over a saucepan of hot water until the mixture is thick and warm. Remove the mixing bowl from the water and continue beating until mixture is cold. Gently fold in the sifted dry ingredients, using a metal spoon. Pour mixture into pan and bake at 375°F for 35-40 minutes. Cool 5 minutes. Turn out on wire rack and wait till cake is cold. Cut into 3 layers. Pit cherries. Heat together ½ cup of the water and sugar in a small saucepan over low heat until sugar has dissolved and then boil until mixture is thick and syrupy. Remove from heat and add half the Kirsch. While still warm sprinkle over cake layers.

Filling. Dissolve the gelatine in the remaining water in a small bowl over a saucepan of hot water. Set aside until cool but not set. Whip the cream until stiff and stir in the remaining Kirsch and the cooled, dissolved gelatin. Sprinkle in sugar to taste. Place one layer on a plate. Spread with thin layer of the cream filling and arrange pitted cherries on top. Reserve a few for decorating the top layer. Cover with the second layer, spread cream filling and cover with third. Spread most of the filling over the top and sides of cake. Coat the sides of the cake with almonds. Sprinkle the top with grated chocolate and top with the remaining cherries.

Chill and serve.

COTTAGE CHEESE TORTE

2 lbs. cottage cheese
¼ lb. butter, melted
2 oranges, juice and
   grated rind

6 fresh eggs separated
2 cup sugar
½ tsp. salt
1 lb. graham wafers

Mix butter, sugar and cheese. Cream well. The cheese should be pressed through a fine seive. Add orange juice and rind. Add well beaten egg yolks and mix well. Beat egg whites dry; add to mixture.

Roll wafers fine and add 2 tbsp. melted butter. Mix well. Butter oblong pan, then add a little more than half of the melted butter and graham wafers on bottom and sides of pan. Add cheese mixture. Sprinkle remainder of crumbs and bake in moderate oven.

WALNUT PETAL TORTE

Bake at 350 degrees for 25 minutes

1 cup sifted flour	**Mocha Cream Filling**
2 tsp. cinnamon	1 cup butter
10 eggs, separated	4 sq. semi sweet chocolate
2 cups sugar	melted and cooled
2 tsp. vanilla	2 egg yolks
2 cups finely chopped walnuts	1½ cup confectioners'
3 cups cream for whipping	sugar, sifted
½ tsp. salt	2 tsp. instant coffee

Grease bottoms of 4 nine inch layer cake pans, line with waxed paper, grease paper.

Measure flour, cinnamon, and salt into a sifter.

Beat egg whites until foamy-white and double in volume in a large bowl. Sprinkle in 1 cup of sugar very slowly, 1 tbsp. at a time, beating all the time until meringue stands in firm peaks. (Beating well will take approx. 20 minutes with an electric mixer). Beat egg yolks in a medium bowl with remaining 1 cup sugar and vanilla until fluffy light. Sift dry ingredients. Beat until well blended. Stir in walnuts, then fold into meringue, until no streaks of white or yellow remain. Pour into prepared pans.

Bake in moderate oven of 350 degrees for 25 minutes until done and centres spring back when lightly pressed with a finger tip.

Cool in pans on wire rack 5 minutes. Loosen around edges with knife, turn out onto racks, pull off wax paper and cool layers completely. Several hours before serving time, make Mocha Cream filling. Put cake layers together with filling between. Beat cream until stiff in a medium sized bowl. Frost top and sides with a thin smooth layer. Place cake on serving plate. Next, taking up spoonfuls of cream on back of teaspoon, press onto cake in rows to make petal shapes. Start at bottom of cake, making one row all the way around and then continuing with second, third, and fourth rows. Finish top same way, working outside to centre. Or frost cake with a thick layer of whipping cream, swirling into peaks with tip of spoon or spatula. Chill until serving time.

For filling: Cream butter until fluffy; beat in cooled chocolate filling slowly, then egg yolks followed by icing sugar and instant coffee.

POPPY SEED TORTE

1 lb. poppy seed, dried and ground
12 eggs separated
1 lb. icing sugar
4 tbsp. bread crumbs or flour
1 cup ground walnuts
1 tsp. vanilla
½ tsp. cream of tarter

Filling and Icing
1 cup butter
1 cup icing sugar
1 cup ground walnuts
3 tbsp. hot milk
1 tsp. vanilla

Beat 12 egg yolks with sugar until lemon colored. Then beat egg whites with cream of tartar until stiff, but not dry. Pour egg yolk mixture over egg whites, stirring very gently with rubber spatula. Mix poppy seeds, crushed walnuts, and bread crumbs together and add to egg mixture. Add vanilla and mix very lightly. Pour into four greased and lightly floured layer cake tins and bake in slow oven, 325 degrees for thirty minutes. Cool layers of cake. Place filling in between layers and ice the torte with the remaining icing.

LOW CALORIE CUPCAKES

1 cup whole wheat flour or white
1 tsp. baking soda
½ tsp. salt
1 tsp. cinnamon
½ tsp. nutmeg
½ cup brown sugar (or honey)

¼ cup shortening
2 eggs, unbeaten
¾ cup buttermilk
1 cup rolled oats
¼ cup raisins or dates

Mix and sift flour, soda, salt and spices into a bowl. Add sugar, shortening, eggs and half buttermilk. Beat until smooth. Fold in remaining buttermilk, rolled oats and raisins. Fill paper cups or greased muffin cups, ½ full.
Bake in moderate oven at 375°F 12-15 minutes or until cakes spring back when touched.

WHIPPED CREAM CUPCAKES

1 cup whipping cream
¼ tsp. salt
2 eggs
2 cups flour

1 cup sugar
2 tsp. baking powder
1 tsp. vanilla

Whip cream until firm, add eggs and whip till light as foam, add sugar, salt and vanilla and beat well. Then beat in flour and baking powder. Bake in muffin tins at 375 degrees, 25-30 minutes. Makes 2 doz. large muffins.

COCONUT PINEAPPLE CUPCAKES

1¾ cups flour
1½ tsp. baking powder
¼ tsp. salt
½ cup shortening
1 cup brown sugar (or white)

2 eggs, beaten
1 tsp. vanilla
½ cup water
½ cup crushed pineapple
1 cup shredded coconut

Cream shortening, sugar and add eggs. Sift flour, baking powder, salt together and add to first egg mixture. Alternately add water, crushed pineapple and coconut. Spoon batter into paper cups (set in muffin tins).
Bake in moderate oven at 375°F, 20-25 minutes.
Makes 24 cupcakes.

SPICED CARROT MUFFINS

1½ cups flour (wholewheat)
1 tsp. baking powder
1 tsp. baking soda
½ tsp. cinnamon
¼ tsp. salt
¼ tsp. nutmeg
1½ cups finely grated carrots
½ cup raisins

½ tsp. each of ginger and allspice
¾ cup brown sugar
1 egg
½ cup buttermilk or
    sour milk
⅓ cup cooking oil
½ tsp. vanilla

Measure dry ingredients into a large bowl. Stir with a fork until well mixed. Whisk or beat together egg, milk, oil and vanilla. Stir in carrots, raisins and nuts. Pour into dry ingredients. Stir just until all ingredients are moist. Batter is quite dry. Do not over mix. Fill muffin cup ⅔ full.
Bake in preheated oven for 15-17 minutes.

WHOLE WHEAT OATMEAL MUFFINS

1 cup whole wheat flour
1 cup rolled oats
1½ tsp. baking powder
1 tsp. baking soda
½ tsp. salt

½ tsp. cinnamon
½ cup brown sugar
1 egg
¼ cup melted butter
1¼ cup buttermilk

Measure dry ingredients into a bowl. Stir with a fork until well blended. Whisk or beat egg with butter and milk. Pour into dry ingredients and stir just until all ingredients are moist. Do not over mix. Fill muffin cups ⅔ full.
Bake in preheated oven 15 minutes.

CARROT SPICED MUFFINS

1½ cups all purpose flour
1 tsp. baking powder
1 tsp. baking soda
½ tsp. each, nutmeg and salt
1 tsp. cinnamon
½ cup raisins
½ cup chopped nuts (optional)

pinch of ginger and allspice
¾ cup sugar or honey
2 eggs
½ cup buttermilk or sour milk
⅓ cup shortening or oil
1½ cups finely grated carrots

Preheat oven to 375°F. Grease or add paper liners to muffin cups. Combine dry ingredients into a bowl. Whisk or beat eggs, milk, shortening. Stir in carrots, raisins. Pour into dry ingredients. Stir just until moist. Batter is quite dry. Fill muffin cups to ⅔ full.
Bake for 15-17 minutes.

1. APRICOT WHOLE WHEAT MUFFINS

½ cup dry apricots
1 cup whole wheat flour
¾ cup all purpose flour
2½ tsp. baking powder
½ tsp. soda
pinch of salt

½ tsp. ginger
½ cup brown sugar or honey
1 egg
¼ cup oil
½ cup milk

Simmer dry apricots till very soft, mash with potato masher. Measure flour, baking powder and soda, salt and ginger and sugar into a large bowl. Stir with a fork. Beat together egg, oil and milk. Stir in cooked apricots. Now combine dry ingredients, mix just until dry ingredients are moist. Fill muffin cups ⅔ full.
Bake in preheated oven for 15 minutes.

PEANUT BUTTER WHOLE WHEAT MUFFINS

1¼ cups whole wheat flour
1 tsp. baking powder
1 tsp. baking soda
½ tsp. salt
½ cup peanuts (optional)

¾ cup brown sugar
1 egg
½ cup peanut butter
1 cup buttermilk
½ tsp. vanilla

Preheat oven to 375°F. Grease or add paper liners to muffin cups. Measure dry ingredients into large bowl. Whisk or beat egg and peanut butter. Add milk and vanilla. Pour into dry ingredients and add nuts. Stir just until ingredients are moist. Fill muffin pan and bake.

BRAN MUFFINS

3 cups shortening
2 cups honey
1 cup brown sugar
8 eggs beaten
8 cups flour plus
   2 cups flour added to
   1-12 oz. pkg. washed raisins

8 cups natural bran
1 quart buttermilk
1 qt. milk
4 tsp. baking soda
4 tsp. salt.
10 tsp. baking powder

Sift dry ingredients, add buttermilk and milk, eggs.
Bake for 35-40 minutes until done at 375°F. These muffins keep well for a long time in the fridge.

2. APRICOT WHOLE WHEAT MUFFINS

14 oz. can apricot halves
5 dried apricot halves
1 cup flour
¾ cup whole wheat flour
2½ tsp. baking powder
½ tsp. baking soda

¾ tsp. salt
½ tsp. ginger
⅓ cup brown sugar
1 egg
¼ cup vegetable oil
½ cup milk

Drain canned apricots very well then put in blender. Measure one cup of puree, set aside. Use scissors to cut dried apricots into tiny pieces. They should measure ¼ cup.
Measure flours, baking powder, soda, salt, ginger, and sugar into a mixing bowl. Stir with a fork until well blended.
Whisk or beat together egg, oil, and milk. Stir in apricot puree and dried apricots. Pour into dry ingredients and stir just until all ingredients are moist. Do not over mix. Fill muffin cups ⅔ full.
Bake in preheated oven for 15 minutes or until done.

GINGER RAISIN MUFFIN (NO EGGS)

¼ cup soft shortening
½ cup well packed brown sugar
1 tsp. salt
½ cup milk & molasses
1 cup raisins

1 tbsp. baking powder
2 tsp. ginger
½ tsp. cinnamon
½ tsp. nutmeg

Mix together:

1 cup whole wheat flour
1 cup all purpose flour

Cream shortening with sugar, salt, mix in milk and molasses. Mix in whole wheat. Sift together remaining flour and spices. Pour liquid ingredients over dry. Stir in raisins and mix just enough to moisten. Spoon into 12 well buttered muffin tins and bake in a 400°F oven about 20 minutes.

MUFFINS

Health Bran Muffins

2 cups bran
2 cups boiling water
2½ cups honey
1 cup shortening
4 eggs
3 tbsp. soda
⅓ cup molasses

1 tsp. salt
4 cups whole wheat flour
1 cup all purpose flour
1 qt. buttermilk or sour milk
4 cups bran flakes
1 small pkg. raisins

Pour 2 cups boiling water over bran and let stand for 15 min. Add all other ingredients and mix thoroughly. Leave in a covered bowl overnight.
Bake in the morning at 350 degrees for 25 minutes.

ꙮꙮꙮꙮꙮꙮꙮ Squares ꙮꙮꙮꙮꙮꙮꙮ

MYSTERY SQUARES

Mix together
1 cup flour
½ tsp. baking powder

½ cup butter
1 egg
2 tbsp. milk

Spread evenly on bottom of pan. Prepare the following mixture for top:

1½ cup sugar (brown)
½ cup coconut
2 eggs
1 cup walnuts

2 tbsp. flour
½ tsp. baking powder
1 cup chopped dates, cooked
rind and juice of 2 small oranges

Spread on crust and bake in moderate oven. When cool, ice with frosting made of icing sugar, juice of orange and butter.

ALMOND BARS

Another Ukrainian pastry; and a luscious almond filling containing mashed potatoes. The pineapple marmalade gives gratifying results. These bars are tasty and delicate in flavor.

2 cups sifted flour
1 tsp. baking powder
½ cup confectioners' sugar
1 tbsp. lemon juice
1 cup sugar
½ cup cold mashed potaotes
¼ tsp. salt
juice of one lemon

¼ tsp. salt
¾ cup butter
2 egg yolks
2 egg whites
1½ cups almonds, blanched
    and ground
½ tsp. almond extract
pineapple marmalade

Sift the flour with the salt and baking powder. Cut in the butter until mixture crumbles in the size of peas. Combine the sugar, egg yolks, and lemon juice. Cream until smooth. Mix lightly with flour mixture; just enough to hold the dough together. Press ¾ of the dough into a buttered 9 x 13 inch pan and reserve the remainder for the top. Bake in a moderate oven of 350 degrees for 10 to 15 minutes. Meanwhile prepare the filling by beating the egg whites until stiff, add the sugar gradually and continue beating. Fold in the remaining ingredients except the marmalade. Spread a thin coat of marmalade over the partially baked crust. Top with almond mixture. Roll the remaining dough into a rectangle and cut into ½ inch strips. Arrange the strips over the filling in a criss cross pattern. Bake in a moderate oven of 325 degrees for 30 to 40 minutes or until set.

MARY'S LIGHT BROWNIES

¼ cup cooking oil
½ tsp. baking powder
1 cup brown sugar
1 tsp. vanilla

¾ cup sifted flour
2 eggs, beaten until lemon color
½ tsp. salt
1 cup chopped nuts

Beat eggs until light, adding oil slowly, while beating eggs. Add sugar, vanilla, salt, flour, and baking powder. Add chopped nuts. Bake until done.

PINEAPPLE BROWNIES

½ cup shortening
2 squares of chocolate, melted
1 cup sugar
2 eggs, well beaten
½ cup well drained,
   crushed pineapple

1 cup sifted flour
½ tsp. vanilla
½ tsp. baking powder
¼ tsp. soda
½ tsp. salt
½ cup chopped walnuts

Mix in order given. Spread and bake for 35 minutes.

BAHAMA BARS

This is a prize winning recipe.

1 cup all purpose flour
¼ tsp. salt
1 egg, beaten

¼ cup brown sugar
1 tsp. baking powder
2 tbsp. milk

Press mixture in a 9 x 9 inch pan which has been well greased. Bake at 350 degrees for 15 minutes

Sift together:
½ cup flour

⅛ tsp. salt
½ tsp. baking powder

Beat 1 egg until light and beat in 1 cup brown sugar slowly until well mixed. Add the sifted flour mixture, 2 tsp. rum flavoring, ½ cup well drained crushed pineapple, and ¾ cup shredded coconut. Blend well.

Spread over base. Return to oven to 350 degrees for 45 minutes.

Cool and cut into bars.

COCONUT SLICE

2 cups flour
1 tsp. baking powder
½ cup butter

1 tbsp. milk
½ tsp. salt
2 egg yolks

Combine and press this mixture in a pan, spread with jam. Spread the following mixture on top:

2 egg whites
½ cup sugar

½ tsp. vanilla
2 cups coconut
butter, the size of a walnut

Bake 25 minutes in a moderate oven.

91

DIANN'S CAKE

½ cup butter
1 cup flaked coconut
1 small pkg. butterscotch
   chips or caramel chips

1 cup chopped walnuts or pecans
1 tin Eagle Brand milk
1 cup graham wafer crumbs
1 small pkg. chocolate chips

Melt butter in a 9 x 13 inch pan. Sprinkle crumbs, over this. Spread coconut, chips, and walnuts over this in the order given. Pour milk over this. Do not stir. Bake 35 minutes at 350 degrees.

PRIZE PINEAPPLE SQUARES

Filling

1 can crushed pineapple
3 tbsp. sugar

5 large apples
2 tbsp. flour

Grate the apples and mix with pineapple, sugar and flour. Boil until thickened.

Dough

4 eggs, separated
   (save whites)
½ cup cooking oil

½ cup sugar
juice of one orange
1 tsp. baking powder

Add enough flour to make dough thick enough to roll. Roll and make two layers, top smaller than bottom. Put bottom layer in a pan about 8 x 10 inches. Put the filling in and cover with second layer. Bake at 350 degrees until brown.

Top Layer

Beat egg whites with 2 tbsp. sugar and 1 tsp. vanilla. Put on top with ½ cup coconut and a few cherries, cut up small. Brown in oven.

CHOCOLATE COCONUT SLICE

1 cup butter
½ cup brown sugar
3 eggs
1 tsp. vanilla
1 cup flour
¼ cup cocoa
½ cup walnuts, chopped

1 can sweetened condensed Eagle
   brand milk
1 cup coconut
2 cups sifted icing sugar
¼ cup cocoa
2 tbsp. butter
3 tbsp. cream

Cream butter and sugar. Add eggs, one at a time, beating well. Add vanilla, sifted flour and ¼ cup cocoa into mixture and blend. Stir in nuts. Spread in a 13 x 9 inch pan and bake for 30 minutes at 250 degrees. Combine condensed milk and coconut and spread on hot cake. Bake until mixture is slightly brown. Sift icing sugar and second cup cocoa in bowl. Add butter, vanilla, and cream well. Spread on warm cake. Cool and cut in squares.

BUTTERSCOTCH SQUARES

½ cup butter, melted
1 egg
¼ tsp. baking powder
¼ cup cherries, chopped

1 cup sugar
¾ cup flour
½ cup chopped nuts
1 tsp. vanilla

Combine ingredients. Put in a greased 8 x 8 inch pan. Bake at 350 degrees for 20 minutes. Ice when cool.

Icing

1 cup brown sugar
4 tbsp. cream

3 tbsp. butter
pinch of salt

Boil together 1 minute. Add 1 tsp. vanilla. Beat with a spoon until spreading consistency.

APRICOT SLICE

1 cup dried apricots, packed
1 cup flour
½ tsp. baking powder
¼ tsp. salt
¼ cup brown sugar

2 eggs, beaten
1 cup brown sugar
½ cup all-purpose flour
½ tsp. vanilla
½ cup chopped nuts
½ cup butter

Cover apricots with cold water and bring to a boil. Turn down heat and boil gently for 10 minutes. Drain and cut into small pieces or mash until smooth. Set aside. Sift flour, baking powder, and salt into a bowl. Add ¼ cup brown sugar and blend with a fork. Add butter and mix. Blend until mixture resembles shortbread. Push into prepared pan and bake 10 minutes. Beat eggs lightly with a fork and add 1 cup brown sugar, ½ cup flour, vanilla, nuts, and apricots. Blend well. Spread on top of dough. Return to oven and bake thirty minutes, or until set.

WALNUT ROLLS

Pastry

2 cups flour
¼ tsp. salt
1 cup butter
4 heaping tbsp. icing sugar
1½ tsp. baking powder
1 tsp. vanilla
¼ to ½ cup milk
Mix like pastry, then add
1 egg

Filling

½ cup walnuts, crushed fine
½ cup brown sugar

Moisten pastry well with cream. Sprinkle with cinnamon. Roll out as you would cookies ⅛ inch thick. Cut in strips, 1½ inches wide by four inches long. Spread with a little of the filling and roll in little rolls. Bake in fairly hot oven until golden brown.

ALMOND MERINGUE SLICE

Boil
¾ cup chopped dates, ½ cup raisins in 1 cup water until soft. Cool.

Add	Add and blend in
½ tsp. cinnamon and mix well	1½ cups flour
Cream together	1 tsp. baking powder
¾ cup butter or margarine	1 tsp. vanilla
½ cup sugar	¼ tsp. salt
1 egg, beaten	3 tbsp. cream or milk

Spread into 9 x 12 inch pan and top with date mixture.

Make meringue of 3 egg whites, 1 cup brown sugar. On top, place ½ cup chopped almonds or walnuts Bake at 350 degrees for 40 minutes.

APPLE BARS

1 cup flour	½ cup butter
½ tsp. salt	2½ cups sliced tart apples
½ tsp. soda	2 tbsp. butter
½ cup brown sugar	¼ cup brown sugar
1 cup oatmeal	1 tsp. cinnamon

Sift the flour with the cinnamon, salt and soda. Add brown sugar. Mix this with oatmeal and cut in the butter until crumbly.

Spread half the mixture in a greased baking dish 7 x 11 inches. Dot it with butter and all sliced apples. Sprinkle the quarter cup brown sugar and cover with remaining mixture. Bake in 350 degrees for 40 to 50 minutes. Cut in bars or squares.

DREAM CAKE

2 cups flour	¼ tsp. salt
2 tsp. baking powder	1 egg, beaten
½ cup butter or shortening	1 tsp. vanilla
2 tsp. sugar	3 tbsp. cream or milk

Roll like pastry. Cover bottom of pan and bake 5 minutes.

3 cups brown sugar	3 eggs, well beaten
1 cup coconut	1½ tbsp. flour
1 cup walnuts	1 tsp. baking powder

Spread mixture over the first cooked mixture and bake until set. When cold, spread with thin icing. Cut into squares.

CARROT SQUARES

4 eggs	2 cups sugar
3 cups shredded carrots	2 cups flour
1 tsp. salt	2 tsp. cinnamon
2 tsp. soda	1 cup oil

Mix in order given; reading across from column to column. Bake in a pan for half an hour.

Icing

1 8 oz. pkg. philadelphia cheese	1 lb. icing sugar
¼ lb. butter	2 tsp. lemon or orange juice
Beat until fluffy.	

POPPY SEED SQUARES

2 cups flour	¼ tsp. salt
2 tsp. baking powder	1 tsp. vanilla
2 egg yolks	3 tbsp. milk or cream
½ cup shortening	2 tbsp. sugar

Cream butter and shortening with sugar. Beat in egg yolks. Add all other ingredients. Spread on cookie sheet.

Topping

3 egg yolks	3 egg whites, beaten stiff
1½ cups brown sugar	1 tbsp. flour
	1 cup scalded poppy seed

Pour over bottom layer. Bake at 350 degrees until brown.

ORANGE WALNUT BARS

Base	Topping
⅓ cup butter	2 eggs
1-4 oz. pkg. white cream cheese	½ cup liquid honey
⅔ cup brown sugar	⅓ cup whole wheat flour
1 cup whole wheat flour	⅓ cup skim milk powder
⅔ cup wheat germ	½ cup walnuts
	¼ tsp. salt
	¼ tsp. grated orange
	1 tsp. cinnamon

Combine the base until you have a dough the consistency of firm shortbread. Press into greased 9 x 13 inch pan. Bake at 350 degrees for 6 minutes.

For topping, beat eggs, honey, 1/3 cup whole wheat flour, skim milk powder, nuts, salt, cinnamon and grated orange rind. Pour topping over evenly and return to oven. Bake about 12 minutes. Cool in pan and cut in squares.

ORANGE COCONUT CHEWS

¼ cup butter
1 cup brown sugar
1 egg
1 cup coconut
1 cup chopped dates

½ cup flour
½ tsp. salt
1 tsp. baking powder
1 tsp. vanilla or orange juice
2 tsp. grated orange rind

Preheat oven to 350 degrees. Melt butter in saucepan. Remove from heat. Stir in brown sugar.

Blend in egg, vanilla, and orange rind. Measure flour, salt, and baking powder onto wax paper. Stir thoroughly. Mix into butter and sugar mixture. Stir in coconut and dates. Spread mixture into greased 7 x 11 inch baking pan.

Bake at 350 degrees for 30 minutes. Cool. Cut into squares. Yields 24 squares.

RUM SQUARES

3½ cups flour
½ cup butter or crisco
4 tbsp. sweet cream

1 cup sugar
2½ tbsp. liquid honey
2 eggs, beaten
1 tsp. baking soda

Cream butter and sugar. Add honey and eggs. Add flour and baking soda. Divide into three equal parts. Roll dough to fit 10 x 15 inch pan. Bake each piece 5 to 8 minutes at 350 degrees. Put pieces together after baking with following:

2 cups milk

4 tbsp. Cream of Wheat cooked until thick and cooled.

Beat in 1 cup butter, 1 cup icing sugar, and 1 tbsp. rum or rum flavoring, also a few drops of food coloring. Ice with chocolate icing. Cut in squares. These freeze well.

COCONUT MACAROON CAKE

½ cup butter
3 egg yolks
1 tsp. baking powder

½ cup brown sugar
1 cup flour
⅛ cup milk

Mix ingredients and press in baking pan. Spread thinly with jam and pour over the following:

½ cup brown sugar
1 tsp. vanilla

1 cup coconut
2 tsp. flour

Beat 3 egg whites stiffly and fold into above. Bake in a slow oven for around 40 minutes.

COCONUT BARS

2 cups brown sugar
1 cup shortening
2 eggs
2 cups oatmeal
2½ cups flour
1 tsp. salt

½ cup coconut
½ cup chopped walnuts
1 tsp. baking powder
1 tsp. soda
1 tsp. cinnamon
1 tsp. vanilla

Cream sugar, shortening and add beaten eggs. Sift together flour, soda, baking powder, salt and cinnamon and add to mixture. Add rest of ingredients. Spread on greased cookie sheet. Bake at 350 degrees for 10 to 12 minutes. Cut into bars. Sprinkle with powdered sugar, if desired.

CHERESHNYANYK CHERRY BARS

2 cups sifted flour
¾ cup sugar
½ tsp. salt
¾ tsp. baking soda
½ cup butter

1 tbsp. lemon juice
½ tsp. grated lemon rind
1 cup sour cream
cherries (1 can pie filling)

Sift the dry ingredients. Cut in the butter. Combine the lemon juice, rind, and cream; add to flour mixture. Mix lightly. This dough should be soft. Spoon or roll batter into a 9 x 14 inch cake pan and pat the side up to hold filling. Fill bottom with cherry filling and crisscross the top wth a little dough left over and bake until light brown. Apple, or any other fruit, is also nice.

COTTAGE CHEESE SLICE

1 cup flour
3 egg yolks
½ cup sugar

1 tsp. baking powder
¼ cup butter
4 tbsp. sweet cream
¼ tsp. salt

Combine. Spread on a lightly greased pan 13 x 9 inches.

Filling

1 lb. dry cottage cheese
½ cup coconut
½ cup sugar

2 egg yolks, beaten
½ cup raisins (washed and dry)
1 tsp. vanilla

Mix all ingredients together and spread over dough. Bake 30 minutes. Cool.

Topping

4 egg whites
½ tsp. baking powder

2 tbsp. sugar
¼ cup crushed walnuts
maraschino cherries

Beat egg whites, gradually add sugar and sifted baking powder. Spread over cake. Sprinkle with walnuts and chopped cherries. Brown in oven. Cut in squares.

Cookies

OATMEAL COOKIES

1 tsp. soda	1 cup butter or lard
2 cups oatmeal	½ cup sour milk
2½ cups flour	1 cup brown sugar

Mix oatmeal, baking soda, butter, sugar, and milk. Roll fairly thin. Cut with cookie cutter and bake at 350 degrees.

Filling

Cut up ½ lb. dates, add enough water to cook until tender. Remove from heat. When cool, add juice, and rind from ½ an orange. Put two cookies together with date filling just when they are to be eaten, leaving them stand with filling will soften them.

LEMON ZUCCHINI COOKIES

1 lemon	2 tbsp lemon juice
¾ cup butter	1½ cups grated zucchini
1¼ cups brown sugar	½ tsp baking soda
1 egg (beaten)	2½ cups flour
½ tsp salt	½ cup chopped walnuts

Grate lemon peel, squeeze out 2 tbsp lemon juice, cream butter, sugar, eggs, add juice, add zucchini, sift flour, soda, salt, stir into creamed mixture, add nuts, drop on cookie sheet. Bake 10-12 minutes 350° F oven.

GINGER SNAPS

1 cup white sugar	2 tsp. baking powder
¾ cup butter	1 tsp. cinnamon
¼ cup molasses	1 tsp. cloves
1 egg	1 tsp. ginger
2 cups flour	pinch of salt

Cream butter and sugar until creamy. Add egg and molasses and beat until blended. Add dry ingredients and mix well. Form into balls and dip them in white sugar. Bake for 10 minutes. The tops of these will always crack.

MELTING MOMENTS

1 cup melted butter	1¼ cup flour
¾ cup brown sugar	1 tsp. soda
1 egg	1 tsp. cream of tartar

Make into small balls and press down with a fork. Bake in hot oven 3 to 4 minutes.

MAGIC SIX WAY COOKIES

1½ cup (1 can) Eagle Brand
  Magic Milk

½ cup peanut butter

Use any one of the six ingredients listed below:

2 cups raisins
2 cups corn flakes
3 cups shredded coconut

2 cups bran flakes
1 cup nut meats, chopped
2 cups chopped dates

Thoroughly blend Eagle Brand milk, peanut butter and only one of the six ingredients listed above. Drop by spoonful on buttered baking sheet. Bake in moderately hot oven, 375 degrees, for fifteen minutes or until a light brown. Remove from pan at once. Makes about thirty cookies.

SOURCREAM COOKIES

2 cups brown sugar
1 cup shortening
2 eggs
1 cup sour cream

½ tsp. nutmeg
1 tsp. soda
4 tsp. baking powder
5½ cups flour

Mix in order given. Mix in flour and drop by spoon on greased pan and bake. Nuts or mixed peel, may be added.

DELIGHTS

½ cup sugar
¾ cup butter
2 eggs, unbeaten

2 cups flour
2 level tsp. baking powder
1 cup raspberry jam
½ cup nuts

Cream sugar and butter thoroughly. Add eggs, flour, and baking powder. Form into balls. Place in small greased muffin tins. Press around the edges of the pan. Fill centre with raspberry jam and nuts. Bake in quick oven about 10 to 15 minutes. When cool, top with whipped cream.

POPPYSEED COOKIES

1 cup butter
1 cup sugar
2 tbsp. cream

¼ tsp. baking soda
2 eggs, well beaten
½ cup poppy seed or currants

Cream butter and sugar. Add well beaten eggs and cream. Sift flour and soda. Put enough flour to make soft dough. Roll and cut with cookie cutter. Bake at 350°F.

SOUR CREAM CHOCOLATE COOKIES

½ cup butter
1 cup brown sugar
1 egg, beaten
1 cup walnuts
2 squares chocolate (melted)

2 cups flour
½ tsp. salt
½ tsp. soda
½ tsp. baking powder
1 tsp. cinnamon
1 cup sour cream

Mix in order given. Drop on cookie sheet. Bake at 375 degrees for 15 minutes.

HOPSCOTCH CRUNCHIES

Melt over hot, but not boiling, water:
1 6-oz. pkg. butterscotch chips   ½ cup peanut butter
Remove from heat and stir in
1 3-oz. (2 cups) chow mein noodles   1 cup miniature marshmallows
Drop by teaspoonful onto waxed paper. Chill until set.

GINGER SNAPS JUST LIKE YOU BUY

1 cup molasses or
  ½ cup syrup and ½ cup
  molasses
2½ tsp. ginger
  flour to stiffen

1 cup sugar
1 cup shortening
2 tsp. baking soda
½ tsp. salt
½ cup boiling water

After combining ingredients, leave for one hour or more. Pinch off bits of dough and roll into balls. Place on a cookie sheet, one inch apart. Bake in a moderate oven.

PINEAPPLE WHOLE WHEAT COOKIES

1 cup pre-sifted white flour
½ tsp. soda
½ tsp. salt
½ cup shredded coconut
¼ cup shortening
1 egg, well beaten

1 cup whole wheat flour
½ tsp. baking powder
½ cup crushed corn flakes
¼ cup butter
1 cup brown sugar
⅔ cup crushed pineapple, drained
1 tsp. almond flavoring

Sift white flour, soda, baking powder, and salt. Add whole wheat flour, coconut, and crushed corn flakes. Blend shortening, butter, sugar, and flavoring together thoroughly. Add eggs and beat well. Alternately, add dry ingredients and pineapple. Drop by spoonful onto greased cookie sheet and bake in oven at 375 degrees, for 12 minutes. Yields 6 dozen.

OATMEAL COOKIES

1 cup butter
1 cup sugar
2 cups oatmeal
½ tsp. salt

1 egg
½ cup sweet milk
2 cups flour
½ tsp. soda
½ tsp. nutmeg

Cream butter and sugar. Add beaten egg and milk. Sift flour with salt, soda, and nutmeg; add to creamed mixture. Add oatmeal and mix well. Roll out on floured board. Cut and bake in moderate oven. When cool, spread filling between cookies. The recipe for filling follows.

Filling for Oatmeal Cookies

1 cup dates
1 tsp. butter

⅓ cup hot water
3 tbsp. orange or lemon juice

Combine ingredients and cook until thick. Cool.

GINGER LACE COOKIES

½ cup molasses
½ cup butter
⅔ cup sugar

1 tsp. ginger
½ tsp. cinnamon
1 cup flour
¼ tsp. salt

Bring molasses to a boil, add butter and let cool. Cream thoroughly, add sugar and spices and mix well. Add flour. Drop by small spoonfuls on a buttered cookie sheet. Place far apart, as they spread. Bake about 12 minutes at 375 degrees and shape into cones while still warm.

UKRAINIAN SUGAR COOKIES

2 cups sugar
1 cup shortening
1 cup sour cream
2 egg yolks
1 whole egg

1½ tsp. baking soda
½ tsp. salt
¾ tsp. nutmeg
flour enough to roll out thin

Cream sugar and shortening. Add beaten eggs and cream. Add sifted dry ingredients using only enough flour so dough can be easily handled. Roll thin; cut into desired shapes; sprinkle with sugar and bake at 350 degrees for about 10 minutes.

FRUIT OATMEAL COOKIES

1 cup shortening	1 tsp. vanilla	2 cups rolled oats
1½ cup brown sugar	2 cups flour	1 cup coconut
2 eggs, well beaten	1 tsp. soda	1 cup walnuts, chopped
½ tsp. salt	3 tsp. baking powder	
1 cup crushed corn flakes		

Cream shortening and sugar. Add beaten egg and vanilla. Mix in dry ingredients. Fold in the rest of the ingredients. Shape into balls. Place on greased cookie sheet and press with a fork. Bake at 375 degrees for 10 to 12 minutes.

PARKINS

2½ cup rolled oats	2 cups sugar	½ cup warm syrup
3 cups flour	1 cup butter	2 eggs, well beaten
4 tsp. soda	1 tsp. salt	1 tsp. allspice
1 tsp. ginger	1 tsp. cinnamon	

Mix all dry ingredients. Rub in butter. When thoroughly mixed, add beaten eggs and warm syrup. Mix well. Make into small balls and bake in moderate oven. Do not flatten these cookies.

SWEDISH PASTRY

½ cup butter	1 egg yolk, slightly beaten
¼ cup brown sugar	1 cup flour
	1 egg white

Cream butter, sugar and add egg yolk. Then add flour. Roll in balls. Dip in egg white (not beaten) and roll in crushed walnuts or coconut. Press in centre and fill with raspberry jam or press a walnut or cherries in centre. Bake until done.

SOUR CREAM COOKIES

2 cups brown sugar	1 cup butter
2 eggs	1 cup sour cream
½ tsp. nutmeg	1 tsp. soda
4 tsp. baking powder	5½ cups flour
	1 cup mixed peel, if desired

Mix in order given. Roll in balls and press with fork. Or, drop from a spoon and bake in oven at 400 degrees until golden.

COCONUT LOGS

1 tbsp. butter
½ cup brown sugar
1 egg

1 cup chopped dates
1 cup chopped walnuts
½ tsp. vanilla

Mix in order given. Roll into shape of logs. Roll in shredded coconut and bake on greased sheet until brown.

BUTTER BUDS

1 cup butter
1 cup brown sugar

2 eggs
2 tsp. vanilla

4 tsp. baking powder
2½ cups flour

Cream butter, sugar, and vanilla. Beat egg and mix with butter. Beat until well mixed. Add sifted baking powder and flour. Drop by spoon on greased pan and bake until done at 350 degrees.

BUTTERSCOTCH COOKIES

1⅞ cups flour
½ tsp. salt
nut meats

½ cup butter
1 cup brown sugar
2 tsp. baking powder

1½ tsp. vanilla
2 eggs

Melt butter. Stir in brown sugar. Add unbeaten egg and vanilla; beat until fluffy. Add flour, baking powder, and salt sifted. Drop by teaspoon onto greased cookie sheet and press the nutmeat on top of each. Bake in moderate oven of 350 degrees, for 8 to 10 minutes.

ANGEL COOKIES

1 cup butter
1 tsp. cream of tartar
pinch of salt

1 tsp. baking soda
1 tsp. vanilla
1 egg

2 cups flour
½ cup each of
brown and white sugar

Cream butter and sugar. Add egg and vanilla. Beat until fluffy. Add dry ingredients, sifted with flour. Roll into balls and press with a fork dipped in sugar. Bake until light brown.

CINNAMON STICKS

1½ cups butter
2 cups sugar

5½ cups flour
1 tsp. cinnamon
3 eggs

Cream butter and sugar; add eggs and beat well until smooth. Add flour and cinnamon and knead well. Chill. Roll out quite thin and cut in strips. Sprinkle with a mixture of sugar and cinnamon. Bake until light brown and crisp at 325 degrees.

DATE PINWHEEL COOKIES

Cookie Dough

2 cups flour	½ cup brown sugar
¼ tsp. soda	½ cup honey
½ cup Crisco	1 egg
¼ tsp. salt	

Measure flour; sift with salt and soda. Cream shortening. Add brown sugar and then honey. Add unbeaten egg to this and beat. Add sifted dry ingredients gradually and mix until smooth. Place dough in a cool place and chill.

Roll out dough into an oblong shape about ¼" thick. Spread with cooled filling and roll as you would a jelly roll. Wrap the roll in wax paper and chill overnight. Next morning, slice and bake on a lightly greased cookie sheet about 12 minutes in a moderate oven.

Filling

The filling should be made and cooled thoroughly before being used to spread on cookie dough.

1½ cups chopped dates	grated rind of one orange
½ cup honey	½ cup orange juice
	dash of salt

Stone the dates and cut coarsely. Combine with honey, orange juice, grated rind, and salt. Cook over low heat until mixture is fairly dry. Remove from heat and set aside to cool.

GINGER SNAPS

This recipe is 100 years old and does not require sugar or eggs.

1 pint Domalo sugar molasses	12 tbsp. hot lard or beef
12 tbsp. hot water	drippings
1 tbsp. ginger	1 tbsp. baking soda

Mix well until it foams. Then mix ½ tsp. salt and 1 tsp. baking powder with a sifter of flour. Add to above mixture enough flour to make a soft dough. Shape into rolls and chill. Slice and bake about 10 minutes in a moderate oven.

KAY'S BUTTER PINWHEELS

½ cup butter	pinch of salt
2 eggs	2 cups flour
1 cup brown sugar	2 tsp. cinnamon
	1 tsp. vanilla

Combine together and chill. In the meantime, cook 1¼ cup dates, 1 cup water, ¼ cup chopped walnuts, 2 tbsp. orange juice. Cook date mixture until it can be spread easily. Cool. Roll dough out and spread evenly with date filling. Roll, slice and bake.

PEANUT BUTTER BALLS

1 tsp. butter
⅓ cup peanut butter
1 cup sifted icing sugar

5 to 6 cherries, cut up
4 squares chocolate
1 cup walnuts, rolled fine

Mix butter, peanut butter, icing sugar, and add cherries. Squeeze into balls. Melt chocolate. Roll balls in chocolate and then in coconut or walnuts.

CHINESE CHEWS

⅔ cup flour
¼ tsp. salt
2 eggs, well beaten
1 cup chopped dates

1 tsp. baking powder
2 tsp. vanilla
¾ cups sugar
1 cup chopped walnuts

Mix and sift flour, baking powder, and salt. Add sugar, nuts, and fruits. Stir in eggs and vanilla. Roll in coconut and drop by spoonfuls on greased pan and bake.

DAD'S COOKIES

1 cup white sugar
½ cup brown sugar
1 cup butter
2 eggs
¾ cup coconut

1 tsp. vanilla
1½ cups rolled oats
1½ cups flour
1 tsp. baking powder
small tsp. soda

Mix in order given and make into balls. Bake at 400 degrees for 10 to 15 minutes.

RAISIN DROPS

2 cups raisins

1 cup water

Boil this for five minutes. Stir in 1 tsp. baking soda.

In another bowl, mix:

3 eggs, well beaten
1 cup shortening, Crisco, or
   butter
2 cups brown sugar
1 tsp. vanilla
½ tsp. salt

1 tsp. baking powder
¼ tsp. nutmeg
1 tsp. cinnamon
1 tsp. mace
3¼ cups flour
1 cup chopped walnuts or peanuts

Mix this with above raisin mixture and drop by teaspoonful onto baking sheet and bake.

MARY'S GINGER SNAPS (CRACKED)

¾ cup shortening
1¼ cup sugar
2 eggs
¾ cup molasses

4 tsp. soda
4 cups flour
1 tsp. cinnamon
2½ tsp. ginger

Mix together. Form ball, but do not press down as they will do so themselves and crack. Bake slowly in oven of 325 to 350 degrees.

BILLY'S OATMEAL COOKIES

1 tsp. soda
2 cups oatmeal
1 cup butter or lard

½ cup sour milk
1 cup brown sugar
2½ cups flour

Mix ingredients together. Roll out thin and cut out. Bake. Make a filling of ½ cup dates, cooked until mushy, add orange rind and orange juice and put between cookies. A nice treat.

MOTHER'S FAVORITE HONEY COOKIES

1 cup honey
1 cup sugar
3 eggs, beaten

1 tsp. vanilla
1 cup flour
1 tsp. baking soda
2 tsp. ginger

Mix everything together. Cover and let stay overnight. In the morning, put two cups of flour in, to make a stiff dough. Make into balls. Dip hands in butter if dough sticks. Bake.

PUDDING POWDER COOKIES

1 cup margarine
1 3-oz. pkg. butterscotch or
  caramel pudding mix
1 large egg
1 cup flour

1 tsp. baking powder
  dash salt
2 cups rolled oats
1 tsp. vanilla

Cream together margarine and pudding mix. Add egg and vanilla. Mix well. Sift flour, baking powder, and salt. Add to creamed mixture and mix well. Blend rolled oats. Form into balls and press with a fork. Bake at 350 degrees for 10 to 12 minutes or until done.

APPLESAUCE COOKIES

1¼ cup flour
1 tsp. baking powder
½ tsp. baking soda
¼ cup milk
1½ cup rolled oats
1 cup applesauce

1 cup sugar
1 tsp. cinnamon
½ tsp. nutmeg
½ tsp. salt
½ cup shortening (Crisco)
1 cup chocolate chips
1 egg

Sift flour, baking powder, and soda together. In a bowl, put milk and oats; mix in applesauce. Add egg, sugar, spices, salt, and shortening. Pour over dry ingredients and mix. Add chips. Drop on greased sheets. Bake at 375 degrees for 15 minutes.

HONEY COOKIES

2 cups brown sugar
2 cups white sugar
2 cups honey
2 cups Crisco
6 eggs
2 tsp. baking soda

1 tsp. salt
1 tsp. cloves
1 tsp. cinnamon
1 tsp. allspice
½ tsp. nutmeg
1 cup sour milk

Mix salt and baking soda with sour milk. Cream sugar, honey, and Crisco. Add beaten eggs and spices. Add milk and flour alternately, using enough flour to make a medium dough. Let dough stand for 3 to 4 hours. Form into balls. Press down with a fork. Bake in a moderate oven.

BRAN COOKIES

½ cup butter
1 cup brown sugar
2 eggs
½ cup sour milk
¼ cup molasses
1 tsp. ginger

1 tsp. lemon extract
1½ cups flour
1 cup bran
1 tsp. baking soda
pinch of salt

Mix together. Place in muffin tins and bake 30 minutes.

Pastry and Pies

DAINTY PYRIZHKY (FILLED PASTRIES)

These dainties have a rich, buttery crust and a luscious fruit nut filling.

1 cup butter	2/3 cup thick strawberry jam
3 egg yolks	½ cup crushed walnuts
2 tbsp. sour cream	½ cup blanched almonds
1 tsp. vanilla	½ cup coconut
¼ tsp. salt	3 egg whites
2 cups sifted flour	

Cream butter with the egg yolks; cream vanilla and salt. Stir in the flour, mix thoroughly, and chill. Combine the jam with the crushed walnuts. Put the almond and coconut through a food chopper. Beat the egg whites until frothy. Break off small pieces of the chilled dough, about the size of a walnut, and roll flat. Fill with jam-walnut filling, seal, and pinch edges together so filling would not come out. Dip in the egg white and roll in the almond-coconut mixture. Place on a baking sheet in a moderate oven of 350 degrees until delicately brown. Yields 72 pyrizhky.

MAKIVNYK POPPY SEED ROLL

Dissolve 1 pkg. dry yeast and 1 tsp. sugar in ¼ cup lukewarm water. Let stand 10 minutes and add ½ cup lukewarm scalded milk and ½ cup sifted flour. Blend ¼ cup butter, ¼ cup sugar, 2 eggs, and ¼ tsp. salt. Add to yeast mixture. Stir in ½ tsp. vanilla, 1 tsp. lemon rind, and 3 cups sifted flour. Knead 10 minutes. Dough will be soft. Put in a greased bowl. Cover with a lid and place in warm place until double in bulk. Punch down and let rise again. Roll out to ¼ inch thickness. Brush with beaten egg white. Spread filling. Roll up. Place on ungreased baking sheet. Let rise. Bake 10 minutes at 350 degrees reduced to 300 degrees for 50 minutes. For sheen, brush top with beaten egg yolk just before it is done.

Filling:

Combine ½ lb. ground poppy seed (or ground nuts), 1 tbsp. lemon rind, 1 tbsp. lemon juice, 1 tbsp. orange juice, ½ cup sugar or honey, and 1 beaten egg.

SOUR CREAM TWIST

Soak 1 pkg. yeast in ¼ cup water

1 cup butter or margarine	4 cups flour
1 tsp. salt	1 cup sour cream
3 eggs, beaten	1 tsp. vanilla
½ tsp. lemon rind	1¾ cups sugar

Dissolve yeast in lukewarm water. Cut butter into flour and salt. Add dissolved yeast, sour cream, eggs, vanilla, and lemon rind. Mix thoroughly. Cover with damp cloth and refrigerate for two hours or overnight. Roll out half the dough on a well sugared board (using ¾ cup). Sprinkle with fillings below. Cut in wedges. Roll wide side to narrow. Put in a pan and rise till double in size. Bake at 400 degrees for 15 minutes.

Fillings for Sour Cream Twist

Walnut Filling

2 cups walnuts, ground	2 egg whites
½ cup sugar	1 tsp. lemon juice

Poppy seed, cinnamon and apple filling could be used. Coconut is another substitute.

KHRUSTYKY (EARS)

6 egg yolks	2 tsp. baking powder
2 eggs	2 tbsp. icing sugar
2 tbsp. cream	1 tsp. vanilla
	flour to make a soft dough

Prepare dough and roll very thin. Cut into diamonds. Make a slit in centre. Push one end, pulling through the slit. Deep fry in hot oil. Drain on paper towel. Sprinkle with icing sugar.

UKRAINIAN PASTRY KHRUSTYKY (EARS)

2 eggs	2 tbsp. rum or brandy
3 egg yolks	1 cup, plus 2 tbsp. sifted flour
2 tbsp. sugar	confectioner's sugar
1 tbsp. rich cream	½ tsp. salt

Beat eggs together until very light. Beat in sugar, cream, salt, and rum or brandy. Stir in flour. This dough should be soft. Cover and let rest for 10 minutes. Roll very thin, 1/8 inch or thinner. Use a small amount of dough at a time and keep the rest covered as it has a tendency to dry quickly. Cut the rolled dough into long strips about 1 ¼ inches wide. Then cut the strips into 2½ to 3 inch lengths crosswise or diagonally. Slit each piece in the centre and pull one end through it to form a loose hoop. Fry, a few at a time in deep fat 375 F. until light brown. Drain. Sprinkle with confectioners sugar.

DOUGHNUTS

2 pkgs. yeast
½ cup warm water
3 cups flour
¾ cup shortening
1 tsp. salt

1 tsp. sugar
6 egg yolks
1½ cups sugar
7 cups flour
4 cups warm milk

Dissolve sugar in warm water, sprinkle the yeast and let stand for 10 minutes. Prepare 3 cups flour, shortening and salt as you would for a pie crust. In another dish, beat eggs and sugar with an egg beater. Add the warm milk, continue beating. Add the yeast and mix in the flour shortening mixture. Gradually mix and knead in the remaining 7 cups of flour. Knead well, cover and let rise in a warm place for an hour. Punch down and let rise till double in bulk. Turn out on a flour board, roll out to about ½" thick. Cut out doughnuts. Let rise for about 1½-2 hours. Fry in oil until done. Drain on absorbent paper. If desired sprinkle with sugar or almond icing sugar or thin chocolate icing sugar.

BASIC SWEET DOUGH FOR DOUGHNUTS OR CINNAMON OR POPPY SEED BUNS

4 cups scalded milk, lukewarm
1½ cups sugar
1 tsp. salt

1 cup butter or margarine
6 egg yolks beaten
2 pkgs. yeast

Dissolve 2 pkgs. yeast in ½ cup warm water and 1 tsp. sugar. Let stand 10 minutes then combine milk, butter, sugar, and eggs. Add enough flour to make soft dough, cover and let rise in warm place until double in bulk. Punch down and let rise again. Knead a few times and let rise once more. Form into a desired shape. This dough is excellent for doughnuts and sweet buns.
Brush buns after baked with ½ cup sugar, dissolved in ¼ cup cream or milk and 1 tsp. almond flavouring. Gives them a nice glaze and flavour.

CREAM PUFF (BUBLYKY)

1 cup water
1 cup sifted flour
½ tsp. salt

⅓ cup cooking oil or
½ cup butter
4 eggs

Bring the water and oil to a boil. Add flour and salt, all at once. Stir briskly until mixture leaves the sides of the pan. Remove from heat. Cool and add unbeaten eggs one at a time, beating hard after each egg is added. Drop batter from a tea-spoon onto an ungreased cookie sheet and bake in a hot oven of 425 degrees for 15 minutes. Reduce temp. to 350 and bake 20 to 25 minutes longer. Small puffs take less time to bake. When cold, make a slit in side of each puff and fill with whipped cream, custard, or ice cream.

SOUR CREAM SCONES

4 cups flour
6 tbsp. Crisco, butter
   or lard
8 tbsp. sugar

½ tsp. salt
1 tsp. baking powder
2 tsp. cream of tartar
2 cups of sour cream
1 egg

Rub flour, Crisco, salt, and all dry ingredients between fingers, like pie crust. Beat eggs and cream together; mix in batter and make a soft dough. Cut with cookie cutter and bake at 375°F until light brown.

POMPUSHKY

3 pkgs. yeast
1 tsp. sugar
2 cups lukewarm water
1 cup scalded milk
¼ cup butter or margarine

4 eggs
1 tsp. salt
10 cups flour
1 cup warm honey
¾ cup oil

Dissolve 1 tsp. of sugar in 1 cup lukewarm water, add the yeast and let stand 10 minutes in a warm place.

In a large bowl, place the flour, making a well in the middle. Beat the eggs and the oil, melted margarine, honey, milk, balance of water and salt. Add this to the flour. Add yeast and mix. Knead in a bowl for 10 minutes. This dough should be soft. Cover and let rise in a warm place until double in bulk. Punch down, knead a few times and let rise again. Take small egg-sized pieces of dough, flatten each or roll ½ inch thick. Place a generous portion of the filling in the centre, bring the edges together and press to seal securely. All the edges must be free of filling. Place pompushky on a lightly floured board and let rise 1 hour. Deep fry in oil for about 3 minutes, turning them to brown evenly on both sides. Drain on absorbent paper.

Poppy Seed Filling

1 cup ground poppy seed
⅓ cup honey
1 tsp. grated lemon rind
1 egg white

Mix poppy seeds, honey and lemon rind in a small bowl. Beat the egg white until stiff and fold into the mixture.

PASTRY

5 cups sifted flour
1 lb. crisco or ½ crisco
   and ½ lard
¼ tsp. baking powder
1 tbsp. vinegar

1 egg
1 tsp. salt
cold water

Beat egg slightly in measuring cup, add 1 tablespoon of vinegar, then fill cup to ¾ full with cold water. Rub shortening into dry ingredients, add cold liquid gradually stirring with a fork. As dough is fairly sticky toss lightly to form a ball when patted together. Store in refrigerator in plenty of wax paper.

SPECIAL PIE CRUST

1 egg
1 tbsp. vinegar
5½ cups flour
1 tsp. baking powder

1 lb. lard
2 tbsp. brown sugar
1 tbsp. salt

Beat egg in measuring cup. Fill measuring cup to ¾ with cold water. Add vinegar set aside. Rub flour, lard, brown sugar, salt and baking powder together with hands. Add liquid all at once and work until smooth. Cover dough with waxed paper and store in refrigerator until ready to use. Bake at 435° — 12 minutes or according to filling recipe.

QUICK TOASTED COCONUT CRUST

2 cups moist toasted coconut
¼ cup melted butter

Combine coconut with melted butter, press evenly over bottom and sides of 6 or 9 inch pie plate. Refrigerate until firm, about 1 hour. Fill with ice cream or fruit. Top with shaved unsweetened chocolate, tinted, plain or toasted coconut or chopped nuts. Yields 6 servings.

CHOCOLATE CORNBREAD CRUST

¼ cup cocoa
½ cup sugar
1 egg
⅓ cup melted margarine

2 tbsp. oil
1 cup milk
1¼ cup cornmeal mix

Add cocoa, sugar, egg, milk and oil to cornmeal mix and mix as for corn bread. Bake at 425 degrees until done. Cool until cold or overnight. Crumble and add melted margarine, press mixture into 9 inch pie pan. Bake 8-10 minutes at 425-450 degrees. Add favorite chocolate pudding or lime pudding and chill.

BUTTERHORNS

1 cup scalded milk,
  cooled
½ cup sugar
½ tsp. salt
½ cup butter

3 eggs, beaten
2 pkgs. dry yeast, dissolved
  in 1 cup water and 2 tsp. sugar
3½-4 cups flour

Knead dough well. Let rise until double; punch down once. Prepare pans. Roll dough and cut into wedges, then roll each wedge individually. Bake at 350°F for 20 minutes. Ice with icing sugar.

CREAM PUMPKIN PIE

1 cup sugar
2 tsp. cornstarch
1 tsp. cinnamon
½ tsp. allspice
½ tsp. ginger

½ tsp. salt
2 cups evaporated milk
1 cup cooked pumpkin
2 eggs, separated
1 baked pastry shell

Mix sugar, cornstarch, spices and salt together, stir in milk and pumpkin. Cook 20 minutes over boiling water, stirring frequently. Remove from heat. Stir into slightly beaten egg yolk. Return to heat, cook 2 minutes longer, stirring constantly. Cool. Pour into pastry shell. Beat egg whites until stiff, fold in small amount of sugar. Spread on top of pie. Bake at 300°F until meringue browns.

VANILLA CREAM PIE

1 pint milk
1 cup sugar
3 egg yolks
4 tbsp. flour

1 tsp. butter
1 tsp. vanilla
¼ tsp. salt

Put milk in double boiler, mix flour, sugar, salt, and beaten yolks all together, beat well, add to boiling milk, add butter and vanilla. Cool, then turn into a baked shell.
Beat whites of eggs until stiff and sweeten with 5 tbsp. sugar. Spread on pie and brown.

BANANA CREAM PIE

Use the filling as Vanilla Cream Pie, but arrange slices of banana on the bottom of the crust. Pour filling over this, then arrange slices of banana over filling. Serve with whipped cream.
Beaten egg white may be blended with hot filling. Makes the filling nice and fluffy.

JAYME'S PUMPKIN PIE

1½ cup pumpkin (canned)
1½ cup brown sugar
½ tsp. salt
1 tsp. ginger

¼ tsp. allspice
3 tbsp. molasses
3 large eggs
1 cup milk

Mix all ingredients well, pour into unbaked 9'' pie shell. Bake at 375 degrees until firm, 55 minutes. Test with a toothpick if it comes out clean, then its done.

JASON'S PUMPKIN PIE

2 cups canned pumpkin
½ cup molasses
1 cup sugar
3 well beaten eggs

1 tbsp. pumpkin pie spice
1½ pt. rich milk or half canned milk
¼ tsp. salt

Mix all ingredients together thoroughly, pour into two or three pastry lined pie pans. Bake at 425 degrees for 15 minutes, then at 325 degrees for about 45 minutes or until a knife inserted comes out clean.

CUSTARD RHUBARB PIE

4 cup rhubarb washed and dried
1½ cup sugar
4-5 tbsp. quick cooking tapioca
6 tbsp. brown sugar

4 eggs, separated
1 tsp. lemon juice
1 tsp. butter

Cook rhubarb with as little water as possible, ¼ cup or less. Add sugar, tapioca, egg yolks, beaten, lemon juice and butter. Pour into unbaked pie shells. Beat egg white until stiff, glossy peaks form. Add brown sugar to meringue; top filling and brown lightly.

1. RHUBARB CREAM PIE

2 tbsp. flour
1 cup sugar
3 cups cut rhubarb

2 well beaten egg yolks
1 cup cream or condensed milk

Blend sugar, flour, egg yolks and cream. Put rhubarb into pie crust. Pour mixture over. Bake at 450 degrees for 15 min. Reduce to 325 degrees until custard sets.

Meringue:

2 egg whites
½ tsp. lemon extract

1 tbsp. sugar

Beat egg whites until stiff. Add sugar, lemon extract. Spoon over pie after baking and bake until golden brown.

STRAWBERRY PIE

1 - 8 oz. cream cheese	1 qt. fresh strawberries
3 tbsp. cornstarch	1 cooked pie shell
1 cup sugar	whipped cream

Wash the strawberries thoroughly, leave half whole and set aside. Crush the remaining half with a potato masher. Add the sugar and cornstarch. Cook until thick, cool. Soften the cream cheese with a small amount of milk or cream to spreading consistency. Spread on the bottom and up the sides of the baked shell. Arrange the whole uncooked berries in the cheese. Pour the cooled, cooked berries over all, chill. Serve with the whipped cream.

APPLE PIE

4 med. tart apples	1 tbsp. lemon juice
⅔ cup brown sugar	1 tbsp. butter
3 tbsp. water	1 tsp. cinnamon

Peel and slice apples into an 8" pie shell. Sprinkle brown sugar, water, lemon juice, butter and cinnamon. Top with a pie crust. Brush milk over crust. Make slits for air to escape. Sprinkle with sugar lightly and bake.

ANGEL PIE

4 egg whites	¼ tsp. cream of tartar
¾ cup sugar	

Beat egg whites until frosty and add cream of tartar. Beat until stiff, but not dry. Gradually add sugar and beat until stiff. Spread in 9" ungreased pie plate. Do not spread too close to the edge of plate. Bake one hour at 300 degrees. Cool.

Filling:

4 egg yolks	1 tsp. grated orange rind
⅛ tsp. salt	1 tsp. grated lemon rind
½ cup sugar	1 cup cream
2 tbsp. orange juice	1 tbsp. lemon juice
2 tbsp. powdered sugar	

Combine egg yolks, sugar, salt, grated orange and lemon rind, and lemon and orange juice and cook in double boiler until thick. Cool. Whip cream and add powdered sugar. Spread half the cream over the cooled meringue crust, then put the cooled filling in and spread the remaining whipped cream over the top. Chill 12-24 hours.

GOOSEBERRY PIE

Pastry:

⅔ cup butter
2 cups flour
1 tsp. baking powder
pinch of cinnamon

2-3 tbsp. ground hazelnuts or
    toasted crumbs
½ cup sugar
1 tbsp. milk or cream

Filling:

1½ lb. gooseberries
1 cup sugar
2 egg whites

½ cup water
1 tbsp. dry bread crumbs

Combine first 8 ingredients for pastry. Mix to a smooth dough, let stand in refrigerator for 5-10 min. Roll out the pastry and line pie pan. Bake crust for 20-25 min., cool. Stem and head the gooseberries, wash thoroughly. Add water and half the sugar. Bring to a boil, simmer very gently 5-10 min. Drain berries, save the juice. Sprinkle crumbs into cooled pastry shell and arrange the gooseberries on top. Beat egg whites in a bowl until stiff. Slowly beat in half of the remaining sugar, until the mixture stands in peaks. Using a metal spoon, fold in the remaining sugar. Put the meringue over the filling. Bake the pie in a pre-heated hot oven, 425° for 3-4 minutes, until the meringue is very lightly browned. Serve warm or cold.
NOTE: the reserved gooseberry juice may be thickened with 1 tsp. arrowroot or 2½ tsp. cornstarch for each cup of juice and poured over fruit.

CHEESE PIE WITH FRUIT TOPPING

Crust:

4 tbsp. butter
1 cup cookie crumbs

1 tsp. vanilla extract
2 tbsp. flour

Filling:

2 cups cottage cheese
½ cup sugar

1 cup cultured sour cream
2 eggs

Topping:

1 cup cultured sour cream
1 tsp. vanilla

2 tbsp. sugar

fresh sugared strawberries, canned or fresh peach slices

To make the crust, melt the butter and mix with the crumbs. Press the mixture into a 9" pie dish. Chill well.
For the filling, blend the cottage cheese, sour cream, sugar, eggs, vanilla and flour together and pour into the crust. Bake in a preheated, moderate oven, 350°F for 20 minutes. Remove from the oven and increase the heat to 450°. For the topping, mix together the sour cream, sugar and vanilla. Spoon onto the partially cooked pie. Place in the oven for 5 minutes or until set. Remove from the oven and cool. Decorate with the peach slices and strawberries.

CRANBERRY AND RAISIN PIE

1 cup cranberries	1 cup raisins, washed
1 cup sugar	1 tbsp. flour
½ tsp. salt	1 tsp. vanilla

Cover cranberries and raisins with water. Cook 20 minutes. Combine sugar, flour, salt and vanilla and add to cooked fruits. Return to heat and cook until thick, stirring constantly. Bake in uncooked pie shell. Cover with lattice top or solid crust.

PLUM PIE WITH ALMONDS

Pastry:

¾ cup butter	pinch of salt
2 cups all purpose flour	2 tsp. grated lemon rind
1 tsp. baking powder	1 tbsp. cream or milk
½ cup sugar	2 egg yolks

To make the pastry, cut the butter into small cubes and place in the refrigerator for 10 min. Sift flour and baking powder. Add the sugar, salt, grated lemon rind, cream and egg yolks. Distribute cubes of butter evenly over flour. Mix to a smooth dough and let stand in a cool place for at least 30 minutes. Roll out the pastry and line the pie pan.

Filling:

¼ cup cookie crumbs	2 lbs. firm purple plums
¼ cup sugar	1 tsp. cinnamon
1 cup flaked, blanched, almonds	

To make the filling, sprinkle the cookie crumbs over the bottom of the pastry shell. Halve and pit the plums. Arrange in circles in the pastry shell and sprinkle with sugar and cinnamon. Sprinkle the almonds over the plums. Bake at 400° for 20 minutes. Lower the heat to 350° and bake for 15 minutes. Serve hot or cold.

STRAWBERRY PIE SUPREME

1 cup sugar	1 cup water
2 tbsp. cornstarch	2 tbsp. strawberry Jello
2 tbsp. white Karo syrup	1 qt. fresh strawberries

Mix sugar and cornstarch, add Karo and water. Bring to a boil and cook for 6 minutes. Add jello and cool. Wash, stem and drain strawberries. Place strawberries in a 9'' baked pie shell. Pour cooled mixture over berries. Store in refrigerator. Serve with whipped cream.

RHUBARB AND RAISIN FILLING

2 cups washed raisins
   (for double crust)
2 cups diced rhubarb
3 cups water
1 cup sugar

4 tbsp. flour
¼ tsp. salt
2 tbsp. butter
¼ tsp. nutmeg

Simmer the raisins in water for 5 minutes. Add the rhubarb. Mix together the sugar, flour and salt. Add the mixture to the boiling raisins and rhubarb all at once. Stir until mixture thickens. Remove from heat. Add the butter and nutmeg. Fill two unbaked pie shells and cover with pastry.
Bake in 400°F oven for 15 minutes, then reduce heat to 375°F for 20 minutes or until done.

2. RHUBARB CREAM PIE

4 cups finely cut rhubarb
1 cup sugar
½ cup flour

¼ tsp. salt
¾ cup cream

Line a deep pie plate with the pastry shell and fill with rhubarb. Mix flour, sugar, salt, and cream together and pour over rhubarb. Bake in moderate oven at 350°F until pastry is a light brown, and rhubarb filling is cooked. This is especially good with any kind of raw fruit. If apples are used, add some cinnamon instead of nutmeg.

RHUBARB STRAWBERRY PIE

1¼ cup sugar
1½ cup water
6 tbsp. cornstarch or
   minute tapioca

2 baked pie shells
6 cups rhubarb
1 cup strawberries

Cook first three ingredients. Add rhubarb being careful not to over cook it. Add strawberries. Cool.
Fill 2 baked pie crusts. Top with whipped cream.

FIRST PRIZE MERINGUE

4 egg whites
⅔ cup sugar

Dash of salt
¼ tsp. cream of tartar

Beat egg whites until bubbly, add salt and cream of tartar and beat until they form slight mounds when beater is raised. Add sugar gradually and beat until mixture stands in moist peaks. Pile on filled pie, sealing edges.
Brown at 375°F. Let cool at room temperature. To serve, dip knife in water after making each cut.

FLUFFY MERINGUE

This does not stick to the knife when cutting.

2 egg whites
1 tbsp. cold water
2 tbsp. sugar

1 tsp. corn starch
½ tsp. baking powder

Beat together 2 egg whites and water until it holds shape. Mix together sugar, cornstarch and baking powder. Stir into egg whites until blended. Cover the pie and bake 15 min. This recipe will cover 2 small or 1 large pie.

PINEAPPLE MARSHMALLOW PIE

½ cup milk
⅛ tsp. salt
1 cup crushed pineapple

½ lb. marshmallows
1 cup whipped cream

Melt marshmallows and milk in top of double boiler, when dissolved, add salt and fold in 1 cup of whipped cream, when cool. Then add crushed pineapple. Put in baked pie shell and top with whipped cream and sprinkle with nuts.

RITZ CRACKER APPLE PIE (Fool your friends)

Pastry for 1 double pie
20 ritz crackers
2 cups water
¼ tsp. nutmeg
1½ cup sugar

2 tsp. cream of tartar
1½ tsp. cinnamon
1 tbsp. butter

Break crackers into large pieces. Cover with boiling water, add sugar, cream of tartar, cinnamon, nutmeg and butter. Pour into pie shell and bake at 350-375 degrees till light golden or until done.

MOLASSES PECAN PIE

3 eggs slightly beaten
½ cup molasses
¾ cup light corn syrup
2 tbsp. butter or margarine, melted

1 tsp. vanilla
1 tbsp. flour
1 cup pecans
1 unbaked 8" pastry shell

Combine eggs, molasses, corn syrup, melted butter, salt and vanilla in mixing bowl. Make a paste of small amount of mixture and flour and stir into remaining mixture. Add pecans. Turn into unbaked pastry shell. Bake at 325 degrees for 1 hour or until firm.

LEMON PIE

3 tbsp. flour
1 cup sugar
⅓ cup lemon juice
2 cups water
Grated rind of one lemon.

3 tbsp. cornstarch
2 eggs
½ tsp. salt
1 tbsp. butter

Mix flour and cornstarch together and blend with a little of the water, then add remaining water and grated lemon rind and cook until thick and clear. Heat yolks with sugar and add to thickened mixture then the lemon juice. Add butter and beat well. Fill previously baked pastry shell and cover with meringue made from two egg whites. Sprinkle with sugar and brown in oven.

MAGICAL COCONUT PIE

4 large eggs
2 cups sugar
2 cups milk
½ cup sifted flour

⅛ tsp. baking powder
½ cup margarine
1 tsp. vanilla
2 cups coconut, fine shred

Beat eggs until light, then add and beat in sugar till thick. Add milk gradually as you beat. Sift together flour, salt, baking powder. Add margarine, vanilla and coconut. Beat or mix well.
Butter 2 eight inch pie plates. Spread evenly and bake at 350°F for 3 minutes or until set. Turn out on plate.

BUTTER TARTS

1 cup currants or sultanas
1 cup brown sugar
2 tbsp. butter

1 egg
½ tsp. nutmeg or vanilla

Clean currants and put into mixing bowl, scald with boiling water, drain, and while currants are still warm, add brown sugar, butter and beaten egg. Stir well together for a few minutes, add vanilla. If the ingredients are mixed together while currants are still warm, there will be a nice butterscotch like syrup.

BUTTERMILK PIE

½ cup butter/margarine
⅔ cup sugar
3 egg yolks
3 tbsp. flour

½ tsp. salt
Grated rind of 1 lemon and juice
2 cups buttermilk, scalded
3 egg whites

Cream butter or margarine and sugar. Add egg yolks one at a time, beating well after each addition. Add flour, salt, lemon rind and juice. Mix well, add hot buttermilk. Beat egg whites until stiff and fold into buttermilk mixture. Pour into unbaked 9-10'' pie shell. Bake at 375°F additional 30 minutes.

RAISIN PIE

Wash 2 cups seedless raisins, cover with water and cook until tender and then cool.

Filling:

¾ cup sugar
1 tbsp. butter
1 tsp. lemon or rum flavoring

2 tbsp. cornstarch
¾ cup boiling water

Add:

2 egg yolks well beaten

½ tsp. salt

Cook until thickens and remove from stove and cool. Into a baked pastry pie shell spread a layer of raisins first, then a layer of filling, then another layer of raisins and lastly a layer of filling on top. Cover with meringue made of the egg whites and brown.

MINCEMEAT

½ lb. finely ground suet
1½ lb. raisins
1½ lb. currants
1½ lbs. brown sugar
1 lb. citron cut in thin slices
   then across in thin strips
1 tbsp. cinnamon

Grated rind and juice of 2 lemons
Grated rind and juice of 2 oranges
1 tbsp. nutmeg
½ tsp. salt
9 apples peeled and cut, coarsely
1 tbsp. mace
1 tbsp. cloves

Add apple cider juice or a blend of fruit juices to moisten, about 5 cups. Grapefruit, orange and apple juice are nice. Bring mixture to boiling point, seal while hot if you wish. To keep over a long period, otherwise store in a cool place in covered crock. Let mature at least 2 weeks.

㏒Canning and Pickles㏒

PICKLED EGGS

12 eggs hard boiled
1 tsp. chopped onion
2 cups vinegar

1 tsp. salt
2 tbsp. horseradish (if desired)
¼ cup of water

Boil eggs till hard boiled. Boil vinegar, water and salt for three minutes and pour hot over eggs in jar, add onions, and seal. Let stand 3 - 4 days.

MUSTARD RELISH

1 large cucumber, cut fine
peel 1 doz. small cucumbers
1 quart onions, cut fine
1 quart small pickling onions

1 large cauliflower, cut fine
1 bunch celery, cut fine
3 red peppers

Put onions, cucumbers, celery and peppers in a dish of warm water with ½ cup salt. Put cauliflower in separate dish and salt. Let this stand overnight and drain off in the morning. Parboil for a few minutes and add to this cooked sauce:

8 cups white sugar
1 qt. vinegar

2 tbsp. white mustard seed
2 tbsp. celery seed

Bring this to a boil and add thickening of:

¾ cup flour   1 tbsp. tumeric   ¼ cup mustard

Moisten with vinegar, thin paste.
Fill jars and seal.

DILLS

Fresh farm cucumbers
(well washed)
Sprigs of fresh dill with seeds.

Horseradish roots
garlic cloves

Wash fresh cucumbers in cold water. In sterilized sealers add cloves of garlic, horseradish root, sprig of fresh dill. Fill sealer with whole cucumbers. Pour hot brine over and seal immediately.

Brine: ½ cup coarse salt, 12 cups water.

Bring to a boil and pour into sealer.

SWEET CUCUMBER RELISH

2 cups chopped onions
12 cups chopped cucumbers
1 large stalk celery, chopped
2 cauliflower cut in fine pieces
3 med. red peppers
1 qt. vinegar

6 cups sugar
2 tbsp. mustard seed
1 tbsp. celery seed
¾ cup flour
½ cup mustard
1 tbsp. tumeric

Chop all the vegetables very fine, (cauliflower, left separately in a dish). Sprinkle all vegetables with ½ cup salt and let stand overnight. In the morning, drain well. Combine vegetables in a kettle, add vinegar, celery seed and mustard seed, optional. Mix sugar, mustard and tumeric, add to flour and stir this well together, moistening with vinegar. Add to the vegetables and cook for 15 minutes. Stirring constantly. Simmer until thickened. Pour into sterilized jars and seal at once.

CORN RELISH

18 cobs corn
2 cups sugar
¼ cup salt
1 tbsp. tumeric

1 tbsp. mustard
1 green pepper
½ cup flour

4 onions
1 cup vinegar
1 tbsp. celery seed

Chop and boil vegetables in ½ cup vinegar. Save the other ½ cup for flour paste for thickening. Mix other ingredients and add to vegetables. Boil till thick.

DUTCH PICKLES

Chop Together:

1 quart peeled cukes
6 small peppers, 3 red,
　3 green

1 small cabbage
1 qt. onion
1 large cauliflower

1 qt. green tomatoes
1 qt. celery

Put salt over the above and pour hot water to cover the mixture. Let stand for ½ hour. Drain.

Prepare dressing:
10 tsp. mustard
1 cup flour

1 qt. vinegar
2 lbs. brown or white sugar

1 tsp. tumeric spice

Boil together about 20 minutes or until done. Pour in sealer and seal.

BEET PICKLES

1 gallon cooked sliced beets
2½ cups brown sugar
½ tsp. whole cloves

2 pints vinegar
1 cinnamon bark

Boil syrup, put sliced beets in boiling syrup to heat up. Pour into sealer and seal. If too sour, weaken with water.

STANDARD DILL PICKLES

This is a standard fermentation method for dill pickles, commonly used by Ukrainian homemakers. Use small or medium sized cucumbers, freshly picked from the garden. Wash them well, cover with cold water and let stand while preparing the sealers. Pack cukes in sterilized quart jars.

Place in each sealer:
Sprigs of fresh dill with seed.
1-2 cloves of garlic
1½ tbsp. coarse salt

Prick the cucumbers with a fork and pack closely into the sealers. Fill with either boiled water cooled to lukewarm or boiling water. When using boiling water, take care not to crack the sealers.

Cover the tops with sprigs of dill and seal. Invert the sealers and shake them to dissolve the salt. If the pickles are to be used soon, keep them at room temperatj re, they will be ready in 4-6 days. For winter, store in a cool place.

DILLS

| 12 cups water | ½ cup salt | ½ cup vinegar |

Boil together and cool. Fill sealers with cucumbers, dill and garlic. Fill sealer with syrup over cucumbers and seal.

Let cucumbers ferment about 7-8 days. Bring water to boil in a canner. Keep sealers in this boiling water just enough to see them turn color. Lift jars out and store. Do not overcook. The heat seals the jars.

DILLS

| 12 cups water | ½ cup brown sugar |
| ½ cup salt | ½ cup vinegar |

Fill the jars with cucumbers; add cloves of garlic and dill to each jar. Pour syrup over cucumbers and seal. Put in a canner filled with boiling water. Keep the jars in until the cucumbers change slightly in color. Take the jars out and store in a cool place.

CARROT MARMALADE

| 3 qts. grated carrots | 4 large oranges |
| 8 lemons, juice extracted and then rinds chopped and ground fine | 1 qt. water added then allowed to stand 24 hours. |

Boil slowly for 1½ hr. Add 1 cup sugar to 1 cup boiled mixture. Add 2 envelopes gelatine. Boil for another ½ hr.
Seal in hot jars.

HEAVENLY JAM

4 large carrots
5 lemons (juice and rind)
5 oranges (juice and rind)

1 doz. peaches
1 doz. apples
10 cups water

Grate carrots and put lemon and orange through fine chopper. Skin and stone the peaches and then mash. Core and finely grate the apples. Boil everything for 1 hour before measuring. To each cup of pulp add 1 cup sugar and boil again, for 2 hours stirring occasionally till it jells.

RHUBARB JAM

5 cups chopped rhubarb
1 cup white sugar

½ orange juice and rind put through chopper

Mix the rhubarb, sugar and orange and let stand overnight. When ready to cook, add 3 cups sugar and cook till syrup is clear (about 30-40 minutes). Then add:

1 package strawberry Jell-o.
1 package frozen strawberries.

Bring to a boil. Bottle and seal.

BEET JELLY

3 cups beet juice
4 - 6 tsp. lemon juice.

1 pkg. Certo crystals

Bring to a boil and then add 4 cups sugar and 1 pkg. jelly powder-strawberry, grape, or raspberry. Boil 6-8 minutes from time liquid starts to boil. Bottle while hot and seal. Very good to serve with meat dishes.

WILD CRANBERRY JELLY

Wash and stem cranberries. Put in a kettle, cover with water. Bring to a boil for 2 - 3 minutes. Strain through jelly bag. Add equal amount of sugar to juice, bring to a boiling point, skim and boil 1 - 2 minutes.
Pour quickly into sterilized glasses and seal.

GREEN TOMATO JAM

2 quarts green tomatoes
1 quart sugar

3 oranges
3 lemons

Slice oranges and lemons and tomatoes very fine. Boil slowly 3-4 hours until dark yellow in color. Pour in hot sterlilized jars and seal.

SASKATOON AND RHUBARB JAM

2 lbs. juicy saskatoons
2 lbs. rhubarb

4 lbs. sugar
1 or 2 pkg. crystal certo.

Clean the rhubarb and cut into ¼ in. pieces, put ½ of the sugar on the rhubarb, overnight and cover the pot. In the morning, put the rhubarb on the stove and put the rest of the sugar in the mix. Cook the rhubarb and in the meantime, mush the saskatoons well, and add to the rhubarb and mix. Add certo and bring to a rolling boil until jam has thickened. Pour into sterilized jars.

VEGETABLE MARROW MARMALADE

12 cups ground marrow
10 cups of sugar
6 oranges

6 lemons
1 tin crushed pineapple
½ cup water

Put marrow through food chopper or place in the pot to cook together with water, for about half hour. Watch so as not to burn. Stir often. Then put oranges and lemons through grinder or food chopper, and add to the marrow juice, peels, sugar and pineapple and cook for 1½ hours longer, or until it thickens. Stir often, especially towards the last hour of cooking. Pour in hot sterilized jars and seal.

CRANBERRY JELLY

1 lb. cranberries
1½ cups sugar

1 cup water

Put cranberries through food mill. Add sugar and water.
Boil together for 15 minutes. Chill until firm.

APRICOT JAM

1 basket apricots 6 lbs.
6 oranges

sugar
large can crushed pineapple

Peel oranges and put the peeling through chopper. Cook gently in small amount of water till tender. Chop orange, pulp and apricot. Remove kernels from 1 cup of stones and chop. Drain crushed pineapple and add to oranges, apricots and orange peel. Measure 1 cup sugar to each cup of fruit. Cook gently for 1 hour until thick. Pour into sterile jars. Then seal tight.

APRICOT JAM

4 lbs. ripe apricots   3 lbs. sugar   juice of one lemon

Place apricots in preserving kettle, sprinkle with sugar, add the lemon juice, mix and let stand overnight.
Boil together until thick, about 20 minutes. Stir to prevent burning. Pour into sterilized jars and seal.

CANNING CHICKEN

Soak chicken in very cold and salty water for 1 - 2 hours. Wash carefully. Place in a large pot of boiling water. Let boil 30 - 45 minutes. Remove meat from kettle. Separate meat from bones and pack into hot sterilized jars, placing largest pieces to the outside of the jar. Put bones back in kettle and reduce the liquid to one half by boiling. Add 1 tsp. salt to each quart jar and pour liquid over. Place sterilized rubber and top in position. Place jars on rack and boil from 1½ to 2 hours.

CANNED CHICKEN

Kill chicken night before. Wash and cut into medium size pieces. Place the pieces of chicken into a large dish, cover with very cold water and pour ¾ cup or more coarse salt. Stir around to dissolve the salt. In the morning wash meat a few times and pack in sealers. Add 1 tsp. salt in each quart. Seal tight and boil 4 hours. Cool.

CANNING SALMON

Wash and cut salmon (fresh) into small pieces and remove bones.
Pack into sealers and put in 1 level tsp. salt. Pack salmon pieces tightly and tighten quart sealer tops.
Put in a boiler of cold water and boil 5 hours. Tighten sealer tops on removing from boiler.
This will stay preserved for one year or more.

CANNING RAINBOW TROUT

Wash and clean fish. Cut all the back bone fat off very well.
Pack pint sealers with trout, add piece of fresh salmon into each sealer. Add 1 tsp. lemon juice.
Boil 3 hours.

CANNING SALMON OR RAINBOW TROUT

Clean and cut into serving pieces. Trout has a strip of fat along the backbone. Remove it carefully. Pack into pint sealers.
Add:

1 tbsp. vinegar	¼ tsp. butter	½ tsp. salt

Seal tight and boil for 3 hours.

CANNING PEAS

1 quart hot water	¼ cup salt	½ cup sugar

Boil above ingredients fast for 5 minutes. Then add 10 cups peas and boil 5 minutes more. Drain, fill pints, put lids on and boil for 1½ hours. Do not put any water in the pints.
Ready for use at any time and will keep for two years done this way.

SAUERKRAUT II

Here is a different method for Sauerkraut, using cooking oil as a protective covering, which helps to exclude air and prevent spoilage.

Shred the cabbage and mix it with chopped onion, carrot and coarse salt. Has to taste quite salty. Pack the mixture into sterilized sealers, leaving a ¾ - 1 inch head space.

Cover with a layer of cooking oil. Seal and store in a cool place.

SAUERKRAUT I

Shred the cabbage and mix it with minced onions and finely chopped carrot. Add enough coarse salt to taste quite salty, allowing 2 teaspoons of salt for 1 pound of cabbage. Mix it thoroughly pressing lightly in hands until the cabbage makes its own juice and appears very moist.

Pack lightly into sterilized sealers adding juice from the Kraut and filling it ¾ full. Fill the rest with boiling water and seal.

The juice in the sealers will run over so put layers of papers on the bottom.

Keep in a warm place. In a 1½ weeks time or so, put sealers in a canner, bring the water in the canner to a boil so the jars get real hot and seal. Take them out and tighten the seals and store. The heating process stops the fermentation.

Icings

HARD SAUCE FROSTING

¼ cup butter
3 cups sifted icing sugar
1 egg

2 tsps. milk
1 tsp. vanilla

Beat until spreading consistency.

EMILY'S FROSTING

¾ cup seedless raisins
6 egg yolks
⅞ cup sugar
¼ tsp. salt
¼ cup rye or bourbon whiskey (wine can also be used)

¾ cup chopped pecans
¾ cup shredded coconut
¾ cup candied cherries, chopped
⅜ cup butter

1. Cover raisins with hot water, let stand a few minutes, then drain and dry.

2. Put egg yolks in top part of double boiler and beat slightly with rotary beater.

3. Add sugar, salt and butter. Put over simmering water and cook, stirring until sugar is dissolved, butter melts and mixture is slightly thickened. Do not over cook. Mixture should be almost translucent. Remove from heat and add whiskey. Beat a minute. Add nuts, raisins, coconut and cherries, mix ingredients, cool and spread between layers and on top.

LUSCIOUS LEMON FROSTING

1 tbsp. grated orange rind
3 tbsp. butter
3 cups confectioners sugar

2 tbsp. lemon juice
1 tbsp. water
Dash of salt

Add orange rind to butter, cream well. Add part of sugar, gradually blending after each addition. Combine lemon juice and water, add to creamed mixture, alternately with remaining sugar, until the consistency to spread. Beat after each addition until smooth. Add salt. Yield: Frosting for 2-9 inch layers.

FAVORITE ICING

5 tbsp. flour
1 cup milk
1 cup white sugar

1 cup shortening
1 tsp. vanilla
cocoa (if desired)

Cook milk and flour until thick. Cool. Cream sugar and shortening, add vanilla. Beat until fluffy, about 15 min. Add to cooked flour mixture. Beat until it looks like whipped cream. Iced cakes may be frozen.

BASIC CREAMY ICING

¼ cup butter or margarine
¼ cup liquid, water, orange juice,
coffee or milk

2 tbsp. peanut butter
2 cups sifted icing sugar
½ tsp. vanilla flavoring

Cream butter or margarine till soft. Add salt, icing sugar, peanut butter and liquid alternately, beating well after each addition. Add flavoring. This quantity will ice an 8 x 12 cake of fill and frost an 8" layer cake.

BROILED COCONUT FROSTING

¼ cup butter, melted
½ cup brown sugar, packed
2 tbsp. milk

¼ cup chopped walnuts
¾ cup shredded or flaked coconut

Combine all ingredients. Spread evenly over cake. Broil until frosting becomes bubbly, 3-5 minutes. Frosts a 9 inch cake.

PEANUT BUTTER ICING

¼ cup butter or margarine
⅓ cup peanut butter
1 egg white

2 cups icing sugar
1 tbsp. cream
½ tsp. lemon juice or orange juice

Cream all ingredients, add enough cream to spreadable consistency. Beat in lemon or orange juice.

BROWN SUGAR FLUFFY FROSTING

Makes enough to fill and frost one 9-inch triple layer cake.

1 package (1 pound) light brown sugar 3 egg whites
1 tablespoon light corn syrup   ¼ cup boiling water
¼ tablespoon cream of tartar   Dash of salt
Dash of ground mace

1. Combine all ingredients in the top boiler, beat until well blended.

2. Place over simmering water, cook, beating constantly with an electric mixer at high speed, 10 minutes or until mixture triples in volume and holds firm marks of beater, remove from heat.

3. Frost cake at once.

SEA FOAM FROSTING

½ cup light brown sugar   ¼ teaspoon of tartar
1 cup granulated sugar   whites of 2 eggs
¼ cup water   ⅛ teaspoon salt
2 tablespoons strong coffee

Boil sugar, water, coffee and cream of tartar without stirring until syrup spins a long thread at 248°F. Pour very slowly over beaten egg whites, beating continually until thick enough to hold its shape, add salt; whip again and spread thickly on cake.

PINEAPPLE NUT ICING

1 large can crushed, pineapple   1 tbsp. butternut flavoring
3 tbsp. cornstarch   1 cup coconut
½ cup butter   1 cup pecans
1 cup sugar   ½ cup maraschino cherries

Cook first five ingredients until thick, add remaining ingredients. Mix well, spread on cake.

SEVEN MINUTE FROSTING

2 egg whites   4 tablespoons cold water
1½ cups white sugar   ½ teaspoon vanilla
1 tablespoon corn syrup   1 tsp. baking powder

Combine all ingredients except vanilla and baking powder in top of double boiler, stir until blended. Cook over bubbling water, beating constantly until frosting is fluffy and holds its shape. This takes about 7 minutes. Remove from heat, add vanilla and baking powder, beat again until the mixture peaks. This will fill and ice a 9" layer cake.

Note: For snow or silver icing, substitute lemon juice for the water.

WHITE MOUNTAIN CREAM FROSTINGS

Makes enough to fill and frost two 9-inch layers.

1 cup sugar
⅓ cup light corn syrup
¼ cup water
4 egg whites

¼ teaspoon salt
⅛ teaspoon cream of tartar
½ teaspoon vanilla

Combine sugar, corn syrup, water and salt in a small saucepan; cover. Heat to boiling: uncover; boil gently until mixture registers 242 degrees on a candy thermometer, or until a small amount of the hot syrup falls threadlike from spoon.

While syrup cooks, beat egg whites with cream of tartar in a large bowl until stiff peaks form when beaters are removed. Pour hot syrup into egg white in a very thin stream, beating all the time at high speed until frosting is stiff and glossy. Beat in vanilla.

Pink Mountain Cream Frosting

Follow above recipe using ¼ cup maraschino cherry liquid in place of water; add few drops red food coloring with vanilla to tint frosting a delicate pink.

DOUBLE BOILER FROSTING

Makes enough to fill and frost three 8 inch layers.

1½ cups sugar
¼ cup water
2 egg whites

2 tablespoons light corn syrup
1 teaspoon vanilla
¼ teaspoon salt

Combine all ingredients in top of a double boiler, beat until blended.

Place over simmering water; cook, beating constantly at high speed with an electric hand or rotary beater, about 7 minutes, or until mixture triples in volume and holds firm peaks from heat.

RUM AND BUTTER CREAM FROSTING

Makes enough to fill and frost two 9 inch layers.

⅓ cup butter
3½ cups sifted confectioners powdered sugar
1½ teaspoon rum extract

¼ cup milk

Beat butter in a medium sized bowl until soft. Add sugar alternately with rum extract and milk until creamy smooth.

Salads

CEASAR SALAD

½ tsp. salt
½ clove garlic
1 ½ qts. salad greens
¼ tsp. pepper

¼ cup salad oil
¼ c. blue cheese (optional)
1 egg yolk lightly beaten
½ c. toasted bread cubes (optional)

Sprinkle salt in wooden bowl, rub garlic over salt. Break greens into bowl. Sprinkle with salt and pepper. Pour oil over greens and toss. Add cheese and lemon juice. Add egg yolk over salad and toss lightly to coat the greens. Add bread cubes and serve immediately.

JELLIED CRANBERRY SALAD

1 cup minced raw cranberries or cooked
½ cup sugar
1-3 oz. pkg. lemon jelly powder
1 cup boiling water

1-10 oz. can crushed pineapple
1 cup chopped celery
½ c. chopped nuts

Dissolve jelly powder in boiling water. Add undrained pineapple and chill until thick. Stir in cranberry mixture, celery and nuts. Pour into a 5 cup greased ring mold and chill until firm. Unmold on serving platter, and if desired fill centre with cottage cheese and a garnish of green pepper. Serves 7 or 8 as a relish.

FRUIT SALAD

1 pkg. lemon pie filling. Cook according to direction on package and let cool.

2 tins fruit cocktail   1 tin mandarin oranges, drain well
1 pkg. marshmallows, cut in quarters or use miniature marshmallows
2 cups whipping cream (well whipped)

Add fruit to marshmallows. Blend gently, add lemon filling and fold in well. Add whipped cream and fold in. Refrigerate 24 hours. Use maraschino cherries and toasted almonds for garnish.

SHRIMP SALAD

1 pint shrimps	lettuce and celery tips
1 head lettuce	pepper and salt
1 hard boiled egg	onions chopped fine.

Strain and wash shrimp, soak in a little water, vinegar, oil and onion. Chop lettuce, slice egg. Place in salad bowl, a layer of shrimp, then a layer of lettuce, season. Spread mayonnaise dressing on salad. Garnish with celery tips and eggs.

FOUR BEAN SALAD

1 can (14 oz.) cut green beans	½ cup green pepper, cut thin
1 can (14 oz.) cut yellow beans	¾ cup onion, sliced thin
1 can (14 oz.) red kidney beans	¾ cup celery, chopped
1 can (14 oz.) lima bean	

Drain beans thoroughly and add remaining ingredients:

¾ cup sugar	⅛ tsp. pepper
½ cup vinegar	1 tsp. celery seed
½ cup cooking oil	celery salt to taste
1 tsp. salt	

Heat oil and vinegar. Add sugar until dissolved. Pour hot mixture over beans and store in a container. Let stand overnight in refrigerator. Stir occasionally to make sure bean mixture is well marinated. To serve, drain sauce from beans but keep this sauce. Any beans left may be returned to sauce and will keep for days in fridge. Makes 12 servings.

CUCUMBER SALAD

1 large cucumber	3 tbsp. water
2 tsp. salt	small onion, sliced
½ cup vinegar	

The cucumber may be peeled or not. If not, simply rinse under cold water and dry. Slice the cucumber very thin. Sprinkle with salt and lightly press by covering with a plate and placing a weight on top. Set aside for 1 hour, then pour away all the juices. Mix together the vinegar and water. Pour over the pressed cucumber slices and allow to stand for 1 hour. Sprinkle with chopped parsley and serve.

CABBAGE SALAD

5 cups finely shredded green cabbage	3 tbsp. lemon juice
⅓ cup olive oil	2 medium cloves of garlic, crushed salt and pepper to taste

Place cabbage in a salad bowl. In a small bowl combine oil, lemon juice, garlic, salt and pepper. Beat with a fork until well blended. Pour over cabbage and mix thoroughly.

CHICKEN SALAD

2 cups diced cooked chicken
1 cup diced celery
½ cup diced cucumber
1 hard cooked egg, chopped

1 tbsp. finely chopped pickles
salt and pepper
½ cup mayonnaise
1 tsp. finely chopped onion

Mix all the ingredients. If time permits, chill the salad. Serve it on crisp lettuce, and garnish with mayonnaise and sliced olives.

MAYONNAISE

½ tsp. salt
½ tsp. dry mustard
½ tsp. sugar
few grains cayenne

2 egg yolks
1 tbsp. lemon juice
1 cup cooking oil
2 tbsp. vinegar

Mix dry ingredients in a deep bowl. Beat in the egg yolks and the lemon juice with a fork or rotary beater. Add ½ cup of the oil, one drop at a time, beating constantly until the mixture thickens. Add the remaining oil and the vinegar, alternately ½ tsp. at a time beating vigorously after each addition until oil had been used. Should the dressing curdle, put 1 egg yolk in another bowl and beat into the curdled mixture gradually until the consistency is smooth. The egg yolk may be replaced with 1 tbsp. of water or vinegar and the mixture beaten into it very gradually. Keep the mayonnaise in a covered container in a cold place.

SPINACH SALAD

1 bunch, about ¾ lb. fresh young spinach
2 tbsp. olive oil
5 bacon strips
1 tsp. herb mixture, a combination
   of rosemary, tarragon and oregano
1 tsp. worcestershire sauce

1 egg boiled hard chopped fine
3 tbsp. apple cider vinegar
1 tsp. sugar
1 tsp. dry mustard
pepper to taste

Wash spinach thoroughly in cold water, drain well and dry excess moisture with paper towels. Tear into bitesize pieces and place in salad bowl. Cut bacon into tiny bits and fry until brown and crisp. Drain off drippings, remove bacon, in the same pan mix olive oil, vinegar, herbs, worcestershire sauce, mustard and sugar. Mix well and heat thoroughly. Add pepper. Toss salad and serve on large plates. Spoon any excess dressing over salad. Sprinkle bacon and egg over top.

SOUR CREAM CABBAGE SLAW

¾ cup dairy sour cream
1 tbsp. vinegar
½ tsp. dill weed
½ tsp. salt

⅛ tsp. pepper
5 cups shredded red and green cabbage
½ c. chopped green pepper

In a small bowl, gently blend sour cream, vinegar and seasoning. Cover and chill. When ready to serve, toss cabbage and green pepper lightly with dressing. Serve with cheese, baked beans.

CABBAGE SALAD FROZEN

6 medium cabbage
4 big onions

6 large carrots

Shred above and stir in 1½ cup sugar. Cook in a pot:

2 cups cooking oil
1 cup sugar
2 tbsp. pickling salt

2 cups vinegar
2 tbsp. celery

Bring to a boil and pour over cabbage mixture and mix well. Let cool. Pack into freezer containers. Make sure the cabbage is covered with brine. To serve thaw, drain off brine.

MAIN COURSE SALAD

1 cup cooked chicken, diced
4 cooked eggs, diced
½ cup chopped celery
2 medium tomatoes cut up
1 tsp. curry powder
2 tsp. salt

1-7 oz. can shrimp
¼ cup water chestnuts, sliced
¼ cup green onions, chopped
¾ cup margarine
2 tsp. lemon juice
2 cups cooked potatoes, pared, cubed

1 can 7 oz. pineapple chunks, drained;
  if in season use ½ lb. seedless grapes, halved.

Combine chicken, shrimp, eggs. water chestnuts, celery, green onions, tomatoes, potatoes, pineapples or grapes in a large bowl. Mix mayonnaise, curry powder and salt in a cup. Pour over above mixture. Toss lightly to mix. Chill several hours before serving. Serves 6.

HOT POTATO SALAD

4 cups sliced cooked potato
3 slices bacon
½ cup chopped onion
½ cup diced celery
2 hard boiled eggs, quartered
8 cherry tomatoes, halved
1 cup spinach leaves
¾ cup flour

pepper
¼ cup vinegar
½ tsp. salt
1 tsp. sugar
1 tsp. dry mustard
1 tbsp. flour
¼ tsp. celery seed

Cook bacon until crisp. Pour off all but 2 tbsp. fat. Cook onion in this fat for 3 minutes. Stir in sugar, salt, mustard, flour, celery, eggs, tomatoes, spinach and crumbled bacon. Heat gently over low heat for 15-25 minutes. Serve immediately. Serve 6.

SALMON PARTY LOG

1 pound can (2 cups) salmon
1 tablespoon lemon juice
¼ tsp. salt
½ cup chopped pecans
3 tbsp. snipped parsley

1-8 oz. package cream cheese, softened
2 tsp. grated onion
1 tsp. prepared horseradish
¼ tsp. liquid smoke flavouring

Drain and flake the salmon, remove skin and bones. Combine salmon with 6 ingredients. Mix thoroughly. Chill several hours Combine pecan and parsley. Shape salmon mixture in 8 x 2 log, roll in nut mixture. Chill well. Serve on crackers.

BANANA WALDORF SALAD

1 diced unpeeled red apple
½ cup diced celery
½ cup mayonnaise or salad dressing
walnut or pecan halves

2 sliced ripe banana
crisp lettuce
salad greens

Mix together apple, celery, mayonnaise or other salad dressing and lightly add banana slices. Arrange on lettuce. Garnish with greens and nuts.

⊒⊒⊒⊒⊒⊒⊒⊒ Dessert ⊒⊒⊒⊒⊒⊒⊒⊒

FRESH PEACH ALMOND UPSIDE DOWN PIE

Pastry for 2 crust 9" pie

2 tbsp. soft butter
2 tbsp. tapioca
¼ tsp. cinnamon
¾ cup brown sugar or
  ¾ cup white sugar

5 cups sliced fresh peaches
½ tsp. nutmeg
⅔ cup toasted, sliced
  almonds or pecans

Line 9" pie pan with 12 inch square of foil — overhang the edge. Spread with butter. Press nuts and ⅓ cup brown sugar into butter. Fit bottom crust into pie pan over nuts and brown sugar. Mix remaining ingredients with ¼ cup brown sugar. Pour into pastry shell. Cover with top crust. Seal, flute, and prick with fork. Brush lightly with milk. Bake at 450 degrees for 10 minutes more. Cool thoroughly. Turn upside down on serving plate; remove foil. Yields six servings.

OLD FASHIONED BAKED RICE

Butter a 9 x 6 inch baking dish and sprinkle in

½ cup regular rice
Add
⅓ to ½ cup sugar
½ tsp. salt
3½ cups milk

1 tsp. vanilla
¼ tsp. nutmeg

Bake at 300°F. for about 2 to 2½ hours, stirring occasionally, until rice is tender and mixture has thickened.

Serves 4 or 5. Serve with cream or ice cream.

NOTE: Add ½ cup raisins and 1 tsp. grated lemon rind if you wish.

Variation: Stir in 1 or 2 egg yolks (beaten) with ¼ cup milk, just before serving, and return to the oven for a few minutes until the rice has a creamy consistency.

2. RICE PUDDING

½ cup rice
½ tsp. salt
¼ cup sugar

2 cups milk
½ tsp. vanilla
¼ cup raisins, (optional)

Wash the rice in cold water.
Cook rice, salt, and milk, over hot water, for 45 minutes or until tender.
Stir occasionally and add more milk if needed.
Add the sugar and raisins and cook 5 minutes longer.
Add vanilla and serve.

BROKEN GLASS DESSERT

2¼ cups Graham wafer crumbs
4½ cups boiling water
1 tsp. vanilla
3 3-oz. pkgs. jelly powder
    red, green, and lemon
1 cup whipped cream

¼ cup brown sugar
1 cup pineapple juice, heated
½ cup melted butter
1 env. unflavored gelatin
¼ cup cold water
¼ cup sugar

Mix Graham wafer crumbs, butter, and sugar together and put in bottom of large pan (13 x 9 inch). Dissolve the three jelly powders in 1 ½ cups boiling water to each package and set each one in pans about ¼ inch thick. When well set, cut in ¼ inch cubes. Dissolve the gelatin in the cold water; add to the hot pineapple juice. Cool until thickened. Whip cream, add sugar gradually, then vanilla. Fold in pineapple mixture and jelly cubes. Pour on top of Graham wafer crust. Let set.

A TROPICAL TREAT

4 cups cornflakes or 1
    cup cornflake crumbs
2 tbsp. sugar
½ tsp. cinnamon
⅓ cup melted butter or
    margarine

15 oz. pkg. coconut cream
    pie filling
1½ cups milk
1 cup whipping cream
½ cup dates cooked in a little
    water
1 14-oz. can crushed pineapple

Combine corn flakes/crumbs, sugar and cinnamon in a 9" pie pan. Add margarine and mix well. With back of tablespoon, press evenly and firmly around sides and bottom of pan. Chill. Prepare coconut cream pie filling as directed on package, using only 1 ½ cups milk. Chill. Whip cream until soft peaks form. Keep ¾ cup aside and fold remainder into cooled coconut cream pie filling along with dates and drained pineapple. Pile mixture into cooled pie shell. Garnish with remaining whipped cream. Chill until firm. Cut into wedges and serve.

GOLDEN BREAD PUDDING

9 - 2 day old bread slices
soft butter or margarine
½ cup raisins (optional)
2½ cups scalded milk

2 well beaten eggs
¼ tsp. each salt and nutmeg
1 tsp. vanilla
½ cup firmly packed brown sugar

Trim crusts from bread or leave on as you wish and spread each slice generously with soft butter or margarine and cut in 4. Arrange a layer, margarine side up in a greased 9 x 6 in deep bake dish. You will need about 3 slices for 1 layer in this sized dish. Sprinkle with a few raisins. Add another layer of bread and raisins. Top with third layer of bread. Combine remaining ingredients and pour over the top. Press down slightly with back of a spoon.

Sprinkle top with a little extra brown sugar and a few shakes of cinnamon. Bake at 350°F for 50-60 minutes or until centre is set and top puffy and brown. Cool slightly and spoon into serving dishes. Serve 6-8. Serve with cream or ice cream.

DEEP DISH APPLE PIE

10-12 tart cooking apples, about 8 cups cut up, or 1 can apple pie filling
1 cup sifted flour or ½ cup flour and ½ cup rolled oats

½ cup brown sugar, packed
2 tablespoons lemon juice

½ cup butter or margarine
1 tsp. cinnamon

Pare apples and cut into small pieces into bowl. Stir in sugar and lemon juice to coat fruit well. Spoon into buttered 9 inch shallow baking dish.

Combine flour, cinnamon and brown sugar in small bowl, cut in butter or margarine with pastry blender, sprinkle over apples, pat down.

Bake in moderate oven, 350 degrees about 45 minutes, or until juice bubbles around edge and topping is golden brown. Serve warm with cream, ice cream or snappy cheese.

PINEAPPLE ANGEL TORTE

1 Angel food cake
1 small can crushed pineapple
Strawberries

1 pkg. instant vanilla pudding
1 pt. whipping cream

Slice cake into three layers. Mix pineapple and vanilla pudding. Let stand for 5 minutes. Whip cream and fold into mixture. Frost between layers, sides and top of cake. Fill centre of cake with a few strawberries. Refrigerate for 24 hours. Yield 24 servings.

1. RICE PUDDING

Wash ⅓ cup rice and place in baking dish.

Add ¼ tsp. salt   4 tbsp. sugar   4 cups milk

Stir to dissolve sugar and place in moderate oven. Cook for about one hour or until rice is cooked. Raisins may be added; and nutmeg or any other spice to taste. Stir occasionally.

BAKED RAISIN LEMON RICE

½ cup seedless raisins   ¼ tsp. salt
2 tbsp. rum or 3 tsp.   2 tbsp. butter
  rum flavoring   2 eggs-separated
1 tsp. lemon juice and rind   ¼ cup sugar
¼ cup long cooking rice
2 cups milk

Wash and drain raisins. Add rum, lemon juice and rind. Let stand 2 hours or overnight. Measure rice, milk and salt in top of double boiler and cook until rice is tender and mixture thickened. Remove form heat and stir in the butter. Add egg yolks, sugar, beat together. Cool. Fold in the raisin mixture and stiffly beaten egg whites. Pour into a greased casserole. Set casserole in a pan of hot water and bake 30 minutes at 325. Serve warm with cream.

MOCK BLACK FOREST CAKE

1 chocolate chiffon cake, or mix   ½ cup sugar
¼ cup kirsch or 2 tbsp.   1 envelope dessert topping mix
  rum flavoring
½ pt. whipping cream
1½ cups sweet black cherries, stemmed and pitted
Grated semi sweet chocolate

Split cake horizontally into three layers. Boil sugar and water together for 2 minutes. Add cherries and cover. Simmer about 6 minutes Chill and drain. Dry the cherries. Reserve the juice and to ⅓ cup juice add the kirsch. Prick the cake layers all over with a skewer. Spoon Kirsch syrup over each. Whip cream until stiff. Prepare dessert topping according to directions. Combine the two mixtures and sweeten to taste. Spread bottom layer of cake with a thick coating of cream and sprinkle with about ⅓ the cherries. Repeat with the next layer. Place third layer on top. Press down lightly. Cover tops and sides with remaining cream. Strew with chocolate and top with cherries. Chill an hour or more before serving.

MY FAVORITE TAPIOCA PUDDING

¼ cup pearl tapioca
2 ¼ cup milk

1 pkg. vanilla pudding

Soak tapioca in cold water for one hour. Cook in double boiler until clear, add more water if needed. Rinse and drain in a collander. Cook vanilla pudding as per directions. Pour cooked tapioca to pudding, mix well. Serve with cream or ice cream.

OLD FASHIONED TAPIOCA PUDDING

¼ cup pearl tapioca
2¼ cups milk
2 eggs slightly beaten

⅓ cup white sugar
Dash of salt
½ tsp. vanilla

Soak tapioca in cold water to cover, for one hour. Add milk, cook in double boiler until clear (about 30 minutes). Beat eggs slightly, add sugar, salt, vanilla and cooked tapioca. Pour into buttered 1½ qts. casserole, place in pan of hot water. Bake in moderate oven until golden brown on top, about 30 minutes. Serve either hot or cold. Serves 6.

STRAWBERRY AND RHUBARB CAKE

2 cups flour
¼ cup sugar
½ cup butter
¼ tsp. salt
1 tsp. baking powder
1 egg beaten

1½ cup sugar
½ cup flour
2 cup rhubarb
1 pkg. 15 oz. frozen strawberries
½ cup melted butter
2 eggs beaten
2 tbsp. minute tapioca

Combine first six ingredients. Reserve one cup for the top and press the rest into 8 x 8 inch pan. Combine the next seven ingredients and pour into pan. Cover with flour mixture, and sprinkle with sugar, cinnamon. Bake in 375 degree oven for 1 hour.

ROCKY ROAD FILLING

¼ c. dark seedless raisins
¼ c. walnuts
1 c. whipping cream
2 tbsp. cocoa

¼ tsp. salt
3 tbsp. sugar
½ tsp. vanilla or rum extract
8-10 marshmallows — cut in pieces

Coarsely chop raisins and nuts. Beat cream to soft peaks, beat in cocoa, salt and sugar. Fold in raisins, walnuts, extract and marshmallows. Yield 9 servings.

COOL FRUIT DELIGHT

1 cup Graham cracker crumbs
4 tbsp. melted butter
or margarine
1 20 oz. container of
sour cream

1 10 oz. bag Kraft miniature
marshmallows — white or colored
1 28 oz. can fruit cocktail,
drained

To prepare crust, combine graham cracker crumbs and sugar, add melted margarine or butter and press mixture on bottom of spring form pan.
Combine miniature marshmallows, fruit cocktail, and sour cream. Blend well, delicately, and pour over crust. Chill several hours or overnight.
Optional: Top pie with maraschino cherries.
Serves 12.

CHERRY DELIGHT

50 crushed Graham wafers
½ cup melted butter
1 large pkg. marshmallows
—colored

½ cup brown sugar
1 pint whipping cream
1 can cherry pie filling

Mix Graham wafers, brown sugar, and butter together and press ⅔ of this on bottom of pan. Pack well. Whip cream and mix with the marshmallows. Put half of this cream mixture onto the crumb mixture. Next, spread with cherry pie filling. Spread remainder of cream mixture over cherries and top with the remaining crumb mixture. Refrigerate overnight.

APPLE CAKE DESSERT

1 can crushed pineapple
½ cup orange juice
1 pkg. unflavored gelatin
½ cup cold water
½ cup sugar
1 cup coconut

½ lb. large or miniature
marshmallows
1 pkg. heavy cream, whipped or
cream substitute
1 loaf angel food cake, sliced into
4 long slices

Drain pineapple, reserving juice. Heat 1 cup pineapple juice and orange juice; add to gelatin, dissolved in cold water. Let cool, add sugar, pineapple, marshmallows, and gelatin mixture to whipped cream. Place in refrigerator and allow to thicken. Place two long slices of cake in bottom of 9 x 15 x 2 inch cake pan. Cover with ½ of whipped cream mixture. Place remaining cake slices on top. Add remaining mixture and top with shredded coconut. Chill several hours or overnight. Colored marshmallows may be used. If using large marshmallows, cut into pieces. Any other type of fruit may be used.

APPLE OATMEAL CRISP

½ cup brown sugar
½ cup all-purpose flour
½ cup rolled oats
½ tsp. cinnamon
½ tsp. salt

½ tsp. nutmeg
½ cup soft butter
1 tbsp. lemon juice
20 oz. apple pie filling

Place apple pie filling (or 4 cups sliced, pared, cored apples) in greased baking dish. Sprinkle lemon juice over apples. Blend the first seven ingredients until crumbly; then spread over apples. Bake at 375 degrees for 25-30 minutes, or until the apples are tender. Serve with cream or ice cream.

RASPBERRY DESSERT

1½ cups crushed graham
   wafer crumbs
⅓ cup melted butter
2 pkgs. Jello
1 pkg. frozen raspberries

½ cup milk
⅓ cup sugar
1 cup boiling water
3 cups miniature marshmallows
2 cups (1 pkg.) Dream Whip

Dissolve the 2 packages Jello in the boiling water. Mix in the frozen raspberries. Spread over crumb base and refrigerate. Melt the marshmallows in the milk in top of double boiler. Cool. Beat Dream Whip and marshmallows. Spread on top of jellied mixture. Refrigerate.

PARTY BISQUE

1 pkg. lemon Jello
1 ¼ cups hot water and juice
   drained from pineapple
⅓ cup sugar
⅛ tsp. salt

1 tsp. lemon rind, grated
1 large tin canned milk
   thoroughly chilled
2 cups rolled graham wafers
1 can crushed pineapple
3 tbsp. lemon juice

Dissolve jelly powder in the hot water and pineapple juice to make 1 ¼ cups. Add sugar, salt, lemon rind, and one tbsp. of the lemon juice. Chill until partly set and then beat until fluffly. Beat the chilled milk with two tbsp. of lemon juice until thick. Fold into jello mixture.
In a shallow pan, about 8" x 12", spread one cup of the graham crumbs. Fill with the jello mixture and sprinkle remaining cup of graham wafers on top. Chill until firm. Cut in squares of desired size to serve.
Approx. 14 servings.
A really delicious dessert at a reasonable cost.

UPSIDE DOWN CAKE

Melt in an 8" square baking pan: 3 tbsp. butter or margarine
Sprinkle with: ½ cup lightly packed brown sugar.
½ cup lightly packed brown sugar
Cover with one of the following:

1. APPLE Slice 3 peeled apples over the sugar mixture.
2. PEACH Arrange 1 - 20 oz. can drained peach slices on sugar mixture.
3. PINEAPPLE Arrange rings over the sugar mixture. Fill centres with cherries or nuts if desired.
4. RHUBARB Increase sugar to ¾ cup. Cover sugar mixture with 2 cups diced rhubarb.

Prepare the following Cottage Pudding-Cream Cake: ⅓ cup shortening, ¾ cup sugar.
Add: 1 egg — 1 tsp. vanilla. Beat until light and fluffy.
Blend or sift: 1¾ cups flour — 3 teaspoons baking powder — ½ tsp. salt
Add to creamed mixture, ¾ cup milk. Mix well pour over fruit mixture.
Bake 350 oven 35 - 45 minutes. Invert at once on a serving plate. Serve warm sauce if desired. About nine servings.

ANGEL CAKE FROSTING AND FILLING

3 boxes whipping cream
9 tbsp. sugar
1 cup miniature marshmallows

1 tall can crushed pineapple, drained
2 boxes frozen strawberries

Whip 1½ boxes whipping cream, add 9 tbsp. sugar. Fold in strawberries, pineapple and marshmallows. Chill. Completely fill cavity of cake with chilled filling. Replace top of cake and press gently. Chill 4-8 hours. After cake has been chilled, whip remaining cream with 9 tbsp. sugar. Spread on cake.

🔲🔲🔲🔲Household Hints🔲🔲🔲🔲

To remove onion from hands, dampen hands and rub with dry mustard, then wash with water.

When making cookies with oatmeal, if the shortening and oatmeal are rubbed together first, then other dry ingredients added, a crisper cookie will result.

In pure Saskatoon pie, a few grains of citric sprinkled in with the sugar mixture will tenderize the berries.

To keep whipped cream from going watery, add icing sugar instead of granulated sugar.

To get more juice from a lemon or orange, first cover with cold water and allow to come to a boil before the fruit is cut, or just roll the fruit to soften a bit.

To keep fruit cake moist and prevent molding, dip several thickness of cheese-cloth in sherry or spirits (not table wine) then squeeze out excess and wrap the cake in cloth and aluminum foil.

To remove odour from jars and bottles, pour a solution of water and soda into them and let stand for several hours.

To keep the odour (or funny smell) out of the refrigerator, make a mixture of 1 cup water, 2 teaspoons soda and spray the freezer part. Wash the fridge with soda and water.

Do not grease sides of a cake pan. How would you like to climb a greased pole?

To moisten brown sugar that has already hardened, place apple slices in container with sugar and cover.

A teaspoon of olive oil added to rinse water for a wool sweater will keep it like new.

To remove a grease spot from a dress, rub cream of tartar on spot, leave a few hours, then brush off.

To remove grass stains from white denim, put wood alcohol on stain, let stand a while, then wash with detergent.

To remove a hot stain from good furniture, rub with a cut raw potato dipped in baking soda.

To clean greasy walls, add 1 cup Spic and Span, ¼ cup turpentine, and ¾ cup milk to 2 gallons of water. This will remove the grease without leaving streaks.

If you want dough to rise quickly, fill the sink with hot water. Put bread dish over sink and allow steam to warm the dough.

Turn your oven on low for a minute, then put your bread or buns to rise in a warm oven. Turn heat off and watch it grow.

METRIC CONVERSION

SPOONS

¼ teaspoon	1 millilitre
½ teaspoon	2 millilitres
1 teaspoon	5 millilitres
2 teaspoons	10 millilitres
1 tablespoon	15 millilitres

CUPS

¼ cup (4T)	50 millilitres
⅓ cup (5⅓ T)	75 millilitres
½ cup (8T)	125 millilitres
⅔ cup (10⅔ T)	150 millilitres
¾ cup (12T)	175 millilitres
1 cup (16T)	250 millilitres
4⅓ cups	1000 millilitres, 1 litre

PANS

8 x 8 in.	20 x 20 cm
9 x 9 in.	22 x 22 cm
9 x 13 in.	22 x 33 cm

OVEN TEMPERATURES

FAHRENHEIT	CELSIUS	FAHRENHEIT	CELSIUS
275°F	140°	375°F	190°
300°F	150°	400°F	200°
325°F	160°	425°F	220°
350°F	180°	450°F	230°

OUNCES — WEIGHT

1 oz.	30 grams	6 oz.	170 grams
2 oz.	55 grams	7 oz.	200 grams
3 oz.	85 grams	8 oz.	250 grams
4 oz.	115 grams	16 oz.	500 grams
5 oz.	140 grams	32 oz.	1000 grams, 1 kg

Simplified Measures

Dash . . . . .Less than ⅛ teaspoon
2 teaspoons. . . . . .1 dessert spoon
3 teaspoons. . . . . .1 tablespoon
16 tablespoons . . . . .1 cup
1 cup . . . . ½ pint
2 cups . . . . .1 pint
2 pints (4 cups). . . . . .1 quart
4 quarts (liquid) . . . . .1 gallon

TRADITIONAL DISHES FOR UKRAINIAN CHRISTMAS EVE — Page 10

Beets and Pedpenky (Mushrooms) 15
Bib 14
Borsch (Beet Soup) 11
Borsch (Beet Soup) 12
Cabbage Roll Meatless, Holubtsi Stuffed 14
Filling for Pyrohy 13
Jellied Fish 12
Kolach, Traditional 15
Kutia (Wheat) 10
Kutia (Wheat) 10
Kutia (Wheat Delicacy) 10
Mashed Beans 14
Mom's Sauerkraut and Peas 11
Pan Fried Fish 13
Pickled Herring 12
Pompushky 16
Pyrohy, Varenyky 13
Sauerkraut and Peas 10
Sauerkraut and Peas, Mom's 11
Stuffed Cabbage Roll Meatless, Holubtsi 14
Stuffed Fish 12
Traditional Kolach 15
Varenyky, Pyrohy 13

EASTER — Page 20

A Successful Babka 21
Babka 21
Babka with Icing Sugar 23
Beet Relish 25
Cheese Cake, Easter Syrnyk 25
Cured Ham 23
Easter Babka, Ukrainian 22
Easter Macaroni Casserole 25
Easter Syrnyk (Cheese Cake) 25
Homemade Sausage 24
Jelly Pigs Feet, Studenetz 25
Kyshka Buckwheat Sausage 23
Mustard Glaze Ham 23
Salchison 24
Sausage, Homemade 24
Studenetz Jelly Pigs Feet 25
Ukrainian Easter Babka 22

SOUPS — Page 26

Borsch (Beet Soup), Standard 27
Borsch Meatless 28
Borsch, Spring Beets. 27
Chicken Soup 27
Chicken Soup with Noodles. 26
Crabapple Borsch, Ken's 26
Dumplings, Old Time. 26
Egg Noodles 26
Ken's Crabapple Borsch. 26
Lloyd's Rhubarb Soup. 28
Manhatten Clam Chowder Soup. 28
Old Time Dumplings 26
Potato and Dumpling Soup. 27
Potato Soup with Gravy. 26
Rhubarb Soup, Lloyd's 28
Spring Beets (Borsch) 27
Standard Borsch (Beet Soup). 27
Vegetable Chowder. 28

MEATS AND CASSEROLES — Page 29

Baked Buckwheat (Kasha) 38
Baked Macaroni and Cheese 32
Baked Macaroni and Weiners 45
Baked Meatballs in Mushroom Gravy 39
Barbecued Sausages 39
Barbecued Spareribs with Garlic, Ken's. 38
Beef Roast 44
Beef Stew 36
Beet Leaf Dough Holubtsi 31
Beet Leaf Holubtsi 30
Broiled Chicken 41
Buckwheat Casserole 35
Buckwheat Filling for Cabbage Rolls. 37
Buckwheat Sausages (Kyshka) 40
Cabbage and Rice Casserole 33
Cabbage Rolls. 30
Cabbage Rolls, Holubtsi 31
Cheese Rolls, Nalysnyky 33
Chicken in Cream, Ukrainian Style 41
Chili Con Carne 40
Chile Con Carne 43
Crunchy Fried Chicken 41
Fried Chicken Livers, Ken's 43

Fried Chicken, Year Round. 34
Herb Fried Chicken 42
Holubtsi, Cabbage Rolls 31
Jellied Pigs Feet (Studenetz) 40
Jiffy Turkey Casserole. 35
Ken's Barbecued Spareribs with Garlic 38
Ken's Fried Chicken Livers 43
Kyshka (Buckwheat Sausages) 40
Lasagna (Sharon's). 44
Liver and Vegetable Casserole. 34
Macaroni and Cheese Loaf 45
Macaroni and Weiners. 39
Meat Balls 36
Meat Loaf 35
Nachinka. 36
Nachinka 37
Nachynka, Cornmeal Casserole 36
Nalysnyky, Cheese Rolls 33
Nalysnyky (Rolled Pancakes) 37
Pepper Steak 43
Perfect Roast Chicken 32
Pork and Mushroom Casserole. 34
Pork Chops Country Style. 38
Pork Chops or Spareribs in Tomato Sauce 33
Pork Hocks or Spareribs and Sauerkraut 35
Potato Pancakes, Lloyd's 33
Pyrogi (Dumplings), Varenyky. 29
Roast Leg of Pork. 42
Roast of Beef with Onion Gravy. 44
Sardines with Sauerkraut. 45
Sauerkraut with Spareribs 32
Sharon's Lasagna 44
Spicy Blade Pot Roast 41
Studenetz, Jellied Pigs Feet 40
Sweet and Sour Spareribs. 45
Swiss Steak 42
Swiss Steak 43
Tasty Spareribs 37
Two Minute Liver Sliver 34
Varenyky (Pyrogi) (Dumplings) 29
Year Round Fried Chicken 34

FISH — Page 46

Baked Haddock, Whole. 50
Baked Stuffed Fish 47

Baked Fish (Pechena Ryba) 46
Clam Chowder 48
Crab Souffle, Hot... 48
Delicious Pan Fried Fish 53
Fish, Baked Stuffed 47
Fish Fillets in Wine.. 46
Fish Fillets in Wine.. 51
Fish, Jellied 47
Fish with Garlic Sauce 52
Fried Pickerel 48
Herring and Mushrooms in Sauce................................. 51
Herring in Cream 53
Hot Crab Souffle 53
Jellied Fish... 47
Lobster.. 49
Nachynena Ryba (Stuffed Fish) 50
Oyster Creamey on Toast... 52
Pan Fried Fish, Delicious... 53
Pechena Ryba, Baked Fish 46
Pickerel, Fried.. 48
Pickled Herring... 49
Pickled Perch 52
Poached Salmon 46
Salmon Cakes 47
Salmon Loaf II 50
Salmon Loaf 50
Salmon Patties 46
Salmon Roll.. 49
Salmon Roll.. 49
Salmon Roll.. 51
Stuffed Fish, Nachynena Ryba 50
Tuna Macaroni Salad.. 48
Tuna Noodles Loaf.. 47
Whole Baked Haddock 50

BREAD AND BUNS — Page 54

Air Buns... 55
Bran and Dried Fruit Loaf.. 60
Bread, Buns, Pyrik and Pyrezky................................... 57
Carrot Loaf 59
Cheese Dumplings 57
Christmas Carrot Loaf... 56
Cinnamon Loaf... 60
Cinnamon Toast 58

Date and Nut Loaf 59
Date Loaf. 59
Four Fruit Bread 56
French Toast 58
Health Bread 55
Hot Cross Buns 58
Overnight Buns 58
Prune Loaf 59
White Bread. 54
White Bread. 54
Whole Wheat Banana Bread 56
Whole Wheat Bread 55

CAKES AND TORTES — Page 61

Applesauce Cake. 61
Applesauce Cake. 62
Apple Torte. 61
Apricot Whole Wheat Muffins 88
Banana Cake 62
Banana Cake 63
Black Cherry Roll 70
Black Forest Cherry Cake 67
Black Forest Cherry Torte 83
Black Forest Torte 82
Boiled Raisin Cake 62
Bran Muffins. 88
Brown Sugar Loaf 76
Butterless, Eggless, Milkless Cake 66
Carrot Cake. 63
Carrot Muffins 63
Carrot Spiced Muffins 87
Cheese Cake 65
Christmas Cake. 80
Christmas Cake, Australian White Fruit Cake 81
Chocolate Cake. 64
Chocolate Filling. 82
Cinnamon Cake 71
Cinnamon Torte 81
Cocoa Cake. 72
Coconut Pineapple Cupcakes 86
Coffee Cake. 64
Cottage Cheese Cake 65
Cottage Cheese Torte 83
Cranberry Carrot Cake 64
Dark Chocolate Cake 77

Easy Cake   71
Eight Minute Cake   68
Frosting for Carrot Cake   63
Fruit Cake   79
Fruit Cake   80
Ginger Raisin Muffin (No Eggs)   88
Jelly Roll   78
Jelly Roll Cake   70
Lane Cake   70
Lazy Daisy Oatmeal Cake   72
Low Carlorie Cupcakes   85
Marshmallow Frosting.   68
Muffins (Health Bran Muffins).   89
Nurses Cake.   71
Orange Cake   74
Orange Chip Cake   75
Orange Chocolate Cake   66
Peanut Butter Whole Wheat Muffins.   87
Poppy Form Cake.   76
Poppy Seed Cake   76
Poppy Seed Torte   82
Poppy Seed Torte   85
Raw Apple Cake   61
Rhubarb Cake.   73
Rich Fruit Christmas Cake   79
Sauerkraut Chocolate Cake.   67
Simple Cherry Cake   66
Sour Cream Cake   75
Sour Cream Chocolate Cake   66
Sour Cream Orange Cake   75
Sour Cream Poppy Seed Cake.   78
Sour Cream Ukrainian Chocolate Cake.   77
Southern Coconut Cake.   74
Special Apple Cake.   69
Spiced Carrot Muffins   86
Three C Cake.   75
Three Layer Poppy Seed Cake   68
Tomato Soup Cake.   74
Walnut Cake   73
Walnut Petal Torte   84
Whipped Cream Cup Cakes   85
White Chocolate Cake   73
Whole Nut Fruit Cake   80
Whole Wheat Oatmeal.   86
Whole Wheat Sour Cream Coffee Cake.   69
Whole Wheat Spice Cake.   78

SQUARES — Page 90

Almond Bars 90
Almond Meringue Slice 94
Apple Bars 94
Apricot Slice 93
Bahama Bars 91
Butterscotch Squares 93
Carrot Squares 95
Chereshnyanyk Cherry Bars 97
Cherry Bars, Chereshnyanyk 97
Chocolate Coconut Slice 92
Coconut Bars 97
Coconut Macaroon Cake 96
Coconut Slice 91
Cottage Cheese Slice 97
Diann's Cake 92
Dream Cake 94
Light Brownies, Mary's 91
Mary's Light Brownies 91
Mystery Squares 90
Orange Coconut Chews 96
Orange Walnut Bars 95
Pineapple Brownies 91
Poppyseed Squares 95
Prize Pineapple Squares 92
Rum Squares 96
Walnut Rolls 93

COOKIES — Page 98

Angel Cookies 103
Applesauce Cookies 107
Billy's Oatmeal Cookies 106
Bran Cookies 107
Butter Buds 103
Butterscotch Cookies 103
Butter Pinwheels, Kay's 104
Chinese Chews 105
Cinnamon Sticks 103
Coconut Logs 103
Dad's Cookies 105
Date Pinwheel Cookies 104
Delights 99
Fruit Oatmeal Cookies 102
Ginger Lace Cookies 101
Ginger Snaps 98

Ginger Snaps 104
Ginger Snaps, Just Like You Buy 100
Ginger Snaps, Mary's. 106
Honey Cookies 107
Honey Cookies, Mother's Favorite 106
Hopscotch Crunchies 100
Kay's Butter Pinwheels 104
Lemon Zucchini Cookies. 98
Magic Six Way Cookies 99
Mary's Ginger Snaps 106
Melting Moments 98
Mother's Favorite Honey Cookies 106
Oatmeal Cookies. 98
Oatmeal Cookies. 101
Oatmeal Cookies, Billy's 106
Parkins. 102
Peanut Butter Balls. 105
Pineapple Whole Wheat Cookies 100
Poppyseed Cookies. 99
Pudding Powder Cookies 106
Raisin Drops 105
Sour Cream Chocolate Cookies 100
Sour Cream Cookies. 99
Sour Cream Cookies. 102
Sugar Cookies, Ukrainian 101
Swedish Pastry 102
Ukrainian Sugar Cookies. 101

PASTRY AND PIES — Page 108

Angel Pie 115
Apple Pie 115
Banana Cream Pie 113
Basic Sweet Dough 110
Butterhorns 113
Buttermilk Pie. 121
Butter Tarts 120
Cheese Pie with Fruit Topping 116
Chocolate Cornbread Crust. 112
Cranberry and Raisin Pie. 117
Cream Puffs 110
Cream Pumpkin Pie 113
Custard Rhubarb Pie 114
Dainty Pyrizhky (Filled Pastries) 108
Doughnuts. 110
First Prize Meringue 118
Fluffy Meringue 119

Gooseberry Pie 114
Jason's Pumpkin Pie 114
Jayme's Pumpkin Pie.. 114
Khrustyky (Ears), Ukrainian Pastry..................... 109
Lemon Pie 120
Magical Coconut Pie 120
Makivnyk Poppy Seed Roll................................ 108
Mincemeat.. 121
Molasses Pecan Pie... 119
Pastry.. 112
Pecan Pie, Molasses 119
Pineapple Marshmallow Pie 119
Plum Pie with Almonds 117
Pompushky... 111
Pumpkin Pie, Jason's.. 114
Pumpkin Pie, Jayme's 114
Quick Toasted Coconut Crust............................. 112
Raisin Pie.. 121
Rhubarb Cream Pie 114
Rhubarb Cream Pie 118
Rhubarb Raisin Filling....................................... 118
Rhubarb Strawberry Pie 118
Ritz Cracker Apple Pie...................................... 119
Sour Cream Scones... 111
Sour Cream Twist... 109
Special Pie Crust.. 112
Strawberry Pie... 115
Strawberry Pie... 117
Ukrainian Pastry Khrustyky (Ears) 109
Vanilla Cream Pie... 113

CANNING AND PICKLES — Page 122

Apricot Jam.. 126
Apricot Jam.. 126
Beet Jelly 125
Beet Pickles 123
Carrot Marmalade 124
Chicken 127
Chicken 127
Cranberry Jelly 126
Corn Relish 123
Dills 124
Dills 124
Dills 124
Dutch Pickles 123
Green Tomato Jam.. 125

Heavenly Jam 125
Mustard Relish 122
Peas 127
Pickled Eggs 122
Rainbow Trout 127
Rhubarb Jam. 125
Salmon. 127
Salmon or Trout 127
Sauerkraut. 128
Sauerkraut. 128
Standard Dill Pickles 124
Sweet Cucumber Relish 123
Vegetable Marrow Marmalade 126
Wild Cranberry Jelly 125

ICINGS — Page 129

Basic Creamy Icing. 130
Broiled Coconut Frosting 130
Brown Sugar Fluffy Frosting. 131
Coconut Frosting, Broiled. 130
Double Boiler Frosting. 132
Emily's Frosting 129
Favorite Icing 130
Hard Sauce Frosting. 129
Lemon Frosting, Luscious. 129
Luscious Lemon Frosting 129
Peanut Butter Icing. 130
Pineapple Nut Icing 131
Pink Mountain Cream Frosting 132
Rum and Butter Cream Frosting. 132
Sea Foam Frosting 131
Seven Minute Frosting 131
White Mountain Cream Frosting 132

SALADS — Page 133

Banana Waldorf Salad. 137
Cabbage Salad. 134
Cabbage Salad. 136
Ceasar Salad 133
Chicken Salad 135
Cranberry Salad, Jellied. 133
Cucumber Salad 134
Four Bean Salad 134
Fruit Salad. 133
Hot Potato Salad 137

Jellied Cranberry Salad 133
Main Course Salad 136
Mayonnaise 135
Potato Salad, Hot 137
Salmon Party Log 137
Shrimp Salad 134
Sour Cream Cabbage Slaw 136
Spinach Salad 135

DESSERTS — Page 138

Angel Cake Frosting and Filling 145
Apple Cake Dessert 143
Apple Oatmeal Crisp 144
Apple Pie, Deep Dish 140
A Tropical Treat 139
Baked Raisin Lemon Rice 141
Baked Rice, Old Fashioned 138
Bread Pudding, Golden 140
Broken Glass Dessert 139
Cherry Delight 143
Cool Fruit Delight 143
Deep Dish Apple Pie 140
Fresh Peach Almond Upside Down Pie 138
Golden Bread Pudding 140
Mock Black Forest Cake 141
My Favorite Tapioca Pudding 142
Old Fashioned Baked Rice 138
Old Fashioned Tapioca Pudding 142
Party Bisque 144
Peach Almond, Upside Down Pie, Fresh 138
Pineapple Angel Torte 140
Raisin Lemon Rice, Baked 141
Rice Pudding 139
Rice Pudding 141
Raspberry Dessert 144
Rocky Road Filling 142
Strawberry and Rhubarb Cake 142
Tapioca Pudding, My Favorite 142
Tapioca Pudding, Old Fashioned 142
Tropical Treat, A 139

BABA's Cook Book —
A GREAT GIFT!

**Ukrainian Orthodox Church of St. Anthony
6103 — 172 Street, Edmonton, AB. Canada
T6M 1C1**

Name ....

Street ....

City ....

Province .... Postal Code ....

Please send .... copies of *"Baba's Cook Book - Volume 1"* at $20.00 each (includes GST, postage and handling. Total amount enclosed: $ ....

Make certified cheque or money order payable to:

St. Anthony's Ukrainian Orthodox Parish.

(Price subject to change)

HAPPY COOKING!

- -

BABA's Cook Book —
A GREAT GIFT!

**Ukrainian Orthodox Church of St. Anthony
6103 — 172 Street, Edmonton, AB. Canada
T6M 1C1**

Name ....

Street ....

City ....

Province .... Postal Code ....

Please send .... copies of *"Baba's Cook Book - Volume 1"* at $20.00 each (includes GST, postage and handling. Total amount enclosed: $ ....

Make certified cheque or money order payable to:

St. Anthony's Ukrainian Orthodox Parish.

(Price subject to change)

HAPPY COOKING!